True Tales of KANSAS

ROGER RINGER

Foreword by Amy Bickle

THE
History
PRESS

Published by The History Press
Charleston, SC
www.historypress.com

First published 2021

Dedication, page 5: "Prairie Dog" Dave Lafferty at Old Cowtown Museum. *Author's collection.*

ISBN 9781540245991

Library of Congress Control Number: 2020945705

In memory of Daniel Ringer, who told me my first stories about farming in Kansas. His son, my grandpa, Lloyd Ringer, we lost when I was young—so many stories lost that I regret every day.

And in memory of my Grandpa and Grandma Becker, who taught me to farm and a lot of other things that I use every day. My first song that I wrote was about how they met at that Grange Hall in Baineville, Kansas—another good story.

And dedicated to my folks, Ronald and Charlotte Ringer.

Special Memoriam to my friend
"Prairie Dog" Dave Lafferty

CONTENTS

FOREWORD

Every Kansan knows about Carry Nation, that hatchet-wielding temperance crusader, as well as John Brown, who fought for Kansas to be a free state. They know about President Dwight D. Eisenhower, a World War II general who grew up in Abilene.

Those stories are in most Kansas history books. However, just beyond what's well known, written about and taught in schools, is a second history—a Sunflower State treasure-trove of fascinating characters and extraordinary events that have, for decades, gone untold or been forgotten, until now.

Some of the best stories of our history are found beyond the margins of textbooks. That's what makes Roger Ringer a unique historian—his ability to find the obscure tales that make Kansas amazing.

Roger is a musician, carpenter, welder, farmer, cowboy, firefighter/EMT and historian who lives near Medicine Lodge. More importantly, he is a lifelong Kansan who loves the state and its people. The reason I enjoy Roger's books is that each book captures stories that, as a historian, you dream of stumbling over. These are stories of whispered scandals, heartwarming yarns and historical lore that have been long forgotten unless you dig deep enough in the archives of the local newspaper or county historical museum.

It's not astonishing that there are so many unknown tales. Kansas, after all, has a rich history that runs deep across its plains. These tried and true tales have been passed down from generation to generation. Roger, however, delivers a few dozen short stories you've never heard before in his latest book, *True Tales of Kansas*. The book takes the reader to all corners of the state with its interesting people and places.

For instance, America's first known female tattoo artist, Maud Wagner, was born in Lyon County in 1877.

H. Truesdell Smith—known as Smitty the Jumper—was an American exhibition parachutist and skydiver who became widely known as the oldest living skydiver, a title he claimed until his death in a Wichita nursing home in 1995.

Amy Loucks was a pioneer medicine woman in her own right. She and her husband, William, homesteaded in sparsely settled Kearny County in 1879. With the nearest doctor seventy-five miles away, Loucks often served as a prairie surgeon and midwife.

Roger finds these stories lost in those yellowed newspapers and dusty county history books and drags them back to the center of the page where they belong.

—Amy Bickel
Kansas journalist and author

AUTHOR'S NOTE

Dear reader: what a ride!

Many years ago, when I started attending rural conferences and agritourism seminars, people knew that I loved history and loved hearing stories. People would come up to me at breaks and say, "I bet you have never heard this story about our town or area." And many times, I hadn't.

I was also performing cowboy poetry and cowboy music and was building a whole new group of friends all over the country. I was busy helping run our family bed-and-breakfast business as well as doing some freelance writing. And then things started to go south. My health started to cut back on my stamina and energy and the ability to travel around Kansas and visit all the neat places that I love so much.

I had a choice to make. I could sit around and feel sorry for myself or do something to keep me occupied and my brain active. I went back to the two years that I worked as an interpreter at Wichita's Old Cowtown Museum. Remembering the stories that I told every day to visitors from all over the world was a fun and fulfilling experience.

I also represented the museum at an event in Oklahoma for the last setting of the marker of the Chisholm Trail, which was a story that I told every day at the museum. The stories of J.R. Mead and Jesse Chisholm, as well as the original Buffalo Bill (Mathewson), were a delight for the historian in me to thrive, especially after one of the museum's historians told me never to hesitate in calling myself a historian because of the knowledge and passion that I had learned starting back in my American history class in high school with a teacher who took the subject seriously.

After working for four years on a manuscript for a book on little-known Kansas and Kansans, I sent an inquiry to the publisher for evaluation. Long story short, here I am on my third book. And the stories keep coming in. I have files and lists of stories that prove that Kansas and Kansans are interesting and worth having their stories saved.

Not all stories are fun or humorous. Many are tragic, and some are downright strange. But all are worth remembering. A true historian is only interested in telling the story as accurately as possible. History is what it is, and there is no excuse to try to change the narrative to judge against our times.

The "official" history texts have long forgotten many of these stories. Even when mandated to be taught in our schools, the Kansas history curriculum is very limited. Popular culture shows that the Kansan is looking to move out of the area or even the entire state. Kansas has had an identity problem since 1910. Before 1910, the Kansan was a gutsy boomer. The state was being sold as a tropical paradise. What it was was a chance for people who never had the chance to start fresh to do so.

Groups of people came and created farms and ranches, and now we feed the world. Farm boys looked to the sky, and we went there. People thought that there were better ways to do things and did them. Even when everything was against them, there was the opportunity to give it your best shot. Many succeeded and many failed. And many failed so many times but got back up and tried again.

I am amazed at how many more stories I find. And I want to tell them all. Sadly, there are stories I want to tell, but there is just not enough material to authenticate. This makes me more determined to find and verify more stories.

As I meet my readers, I am delighted at the reception that my books are getting. Good Lord willing and the creeks don't rise, I will keep researching and writing about this resilient group of people known as KANSANS.

—The Author

TRUE TALES OF KANSAS

ROOKS COUNTY TRAGEDY, FOUR CHILDREN BURNED

Life on the prairie was never easy under any circumstances. Tragedies were very common, but the tragedy that happened in a soddy just inside the line in Rooks County in December 1904 was one of the worst. On Bow Creek at the homestead of C.H. Smith, Mr. Smith and his wife took two wagons of corn and headed toward Stockton, leaving the children at home with the fourteen-year-old, Lily Locey, in charge. Lily was the oldest and from the first marriage of Mrs. Smith. There were two younger girls and a boy.

The four children were in the home, and the fire had died down in the stove. It was decided to get the fire going in the stove again, and the five-year-old, Neva, took a can of kerosene and poured the contents on the ashes in the stove. But the ashes had not gone out completely, and when a match was struck, the stove exploded, filling the soddy with flames. Being next to the boy, Lily grabbed him by his flaming clothing and rushed him outside by the well. She put out the fire in a tub of water and snow and went back into the burning house.

Lily carried both of the other flaming children outside and put them in the barn, covered them with a blanket and went in and pulled out several pieces of furniture. By this time, the clothing had been burned off poor Lily, who had rolled in the snow to put herself out. But she knew she had to go get help. The children were writhing in agony, and the courageous Lily started down the road to get help.

Lily ran into Dan McGee, who was shucking corn about a mile away. He put the burned and naked Lily in his wagon and drove a quarter of a mile to his father's home. By the time they got poor Lily into the home, her flesh was dropping off her body. Word was sent to Dr. R.J. Dickerson of Kirwin, but it was after noon before he could arrive.

The men drove back to the Smith place, and it was a gruesome sight that awaited them. The younger girl, Neva, who had put the kerosene in the stove, had her eyes burned from her sockets and the flesh and muscle had sloughed off the bones in several places.

The parents were caught up to about two miles from Stockton and could not believe that such a terrible thing had happened. They were brought back home in a carriage to be horrified by what they found.

There was no medical skill that could do anything but try to ease some pain. The two younger girls died that day, but Lily lingered until the following Monday and was able to relate what had happened. The boy, Charlie, the first child Lily had removed from the burning house, survived into adulthood. The children are buried in the Bow Creek Cemetery at Glade in Phillips County.

Fire has always been a fact of life in Kansas, but when it strikes so many so horribly, it is an event that needs to be remembered.

COTTONWOOD DAVIS

Charles Wood Davis (Cottonwood Davis) is an important figure in Kansas history in both Sedgwick and Crawford Counties. But the story of Cottonwood's life starts long before he came to Kansas. Cottonwood was not only involved in railroads, coal and water, but he was also a pioneer in many ways before coming to the Kansas frontier.

The Davis family was involved in the American Revolution; a member of the family was the first man killed at Lexington. Cottonwood had a brother, an officer in the Twelfth Michigan Volunteer Infantry, killed at the Battle of Shiloh on April 6, 1863. The Davis family was in the shipbuilding industry in New England, and he was educated in the common schools of the region.

At age sixteen, Cottonwood signed on a ship and sailed from New Bedford, Massachusetts, as a cabin boy. He discovered a fire onboard and was the first to fight the fire and raise the alarm. Acting as a nurse to injured sailors and through outstanding service, he worked his way up to be first mate. After sailing on two or three merchant vessels and having circumnavigated the globe, he joined in the adventure of being on the first ship to sail around Cape Horn, sailing up the west coast of South and North America to join the gold rush in 1849.

Cottonwood was successful in the gold fields and built a big hotel in San Francisco. After the completion of the hotel, he set sail back to New Bedford. Shortly after his arrival, the hotel he built burned to the ground.

On December 5, 1851, he married Miss Sarah F. Rowe, and they settled in Detroit, Michigan. There he assumed the position of check clerk for the Michigan Central Railroad Company. His business acumen won him rapid promotion in the company, and he finally became an auditor. His organization of freight scheduling at Michigan Central became a standard that is still used today. He worked there for fourteen years.

Through the influence of General John C. Frémont, he became a traffic manager for the Kansas Pacific Railroad. He held this position for three years and then, due to ill health, retired and settled in Saline County, Kansas, and turned to drilling a salt well. Drilling to a depth of six hundred feet, he found a strong flow of salt water, which he flowed into vats and evaporated the water, producing salt. His was the first commercial salt enterprise in Kansas.

In 1870, he acquired a farm in the Clear Creek Valley of the Ninnescah River north of what is now the town of Viola. Cottonwood was the first to settle in the area and built the first frame farmhouse. His son Charles G. Davis incorporated the Township of Viola around 1876, making it the first organized township in Sedgwick County.

Cottonwood also moved to Crawford County, where he was involved in an independent coal mining operation. The first shaft was located at what are now Broadway and South First Street in Pittsburg. He had been superintendent for the Oswego Coal Company and with partners Major Rombauer and Charles Patmor formed the Pittsburg Coal Company. The company faced the same problem that other independent coal miners faced in that they could not get rail cars to transport their coal. Cottonwood succeeded in getting the Gulf Railroad to extend a line from Minden through Pittsburg. Even with the new access to rail transport, the company fell on hard times and was forced into bankruptcy. The reorganized company, known as the Pittsburg & Midway Company, was formed and the shaft moved to Midway, north of Pittsburg.

In 1889, Cottonwood returned to his home in Viola Township. He was a force in getting the Frisco Railway to extend from Oswego to Wichita and later induced the Chicago & Rock Island to extend its line into Kansas.

Charles "Cottonwood" Davis. *Courtesy of Martha Brohammer.*

Cottonwood also had the distinction of being one of the men "who stood under the Oaks" at Jackson, Michigan, which affected the organization of the Republican Party. He was a delegate at the convention that nominated Abraham Lincoln for the presidency. In 1890–92, he was in Washington in the interest of the "anti-option bill," which failed to be enacted. He was an expert on crops and was mentioned in papers and published in periodicals and newspapers as the "greatest grain statesman in the world." He died in 1910.

FRIED CHICKEN

Throughout Kansas history, there is one thing that is consistent: people need to eat. Also, when hard times hit for whatever reason, the way many responded was to open a café or restaurant. One thing that people really love is fried chicken. Southeast Kansas has seen its hard times as much as or more than any other part of the state, and the result has been people doing what they could to make a living and ending up with a legacy that has been handed down through the generations. When you say *fried chicken*, what comes to mind is either Chicken Annie's or Chicken Mary's. But there are more that have taken on legendary status in the southeastern part of the state, each with an interesting and compelling story. In order to cover all of them in *8 Wonders of Kansas Guidebook*, Marci Penner listed them together as "Crawford County Fried Chicken."

So here is a quick story of each: Annie Pritcher was married to a miner who worked in various mines in the area. Her husband, Charley, was injured in a mine accident in March 1933 at the Western Mine. One leg was severely crushed and the other had to be amputated below the knee. Now the job of making the living fell on Annie. Annie raised chickens and had a garden in which she raised peppers and pickled them. After working a short time as a seamstress with the WPA, she started to sell ham and veal sandwiches for fifteen cents with a home-brew thrown in. She started serving fried chicken in a small way. They started in the home, and Charley would help cook. The business grew and grew. The main meal was fried chicken, German potato salad, coleslaw and a strip of pickled pepper. By 1963, Annie had retired and let the children continue in the business. A new building was constructed, and Chicken Annie's is still in business across from the old Pitcher place.

Joe and Mary Zemgast started Chicken Mary's just down the road from Chicken Annie's. In a similar circumstance, Mary's husband was a miner

This page: Chicken Mary's today. *Courtesy of Nick Anderson.*

The original Chicken Annie's. *Courtesy of the Kansas State Historical Society.*

and ended up in bad health. In order to survive, Mary did what she knew best, which was cooking. She also fried chicken and served German potato salad and coleslaw. They started serving people in the front room of the house, and there were no set hours. As someone knocked on the door, they would start preparing a hot meal. Nearby was the Foxtown Mining Camp Pool Hall, which was a rowdy place. At the prompting of area folks, the Zemgasts purchased the building and moved it next to the house, turning it into Chicken Mary's. Joe died in 1960, but Mary's son and his wife continued to run the place until Mary suffered a stroke. The business closed for six months and then opened on a limited basis. Today, the restaurant is running with a very loyal staff and is still family owned.

Gebhardt's Chicken and Dinners is not far away in Mulberry. Ted Gebhardt came home from the army in 1942 and married Maycle, and then they moved back to the farm. Ted purchased the Little Honky Tonk Bar next to the farm and ran that for a while. They decided the bar was not the atmosphere that they wanted to raise their family around and turned it into a restaurant on September 16, 1946. Their daughter Meg was involved, and her Aunt Tessie and Grandmother Margret put recipes together. The restaurant was open seven days a week while Ted farmed full time. Ted was killed in an auto accident in 1999. Meg and Maycle took over operations.

Barto's Idle Hour in Frontenac was opened by Ray Barto in the early 1950s in what he described as "a need to provide weekend entertainment." The signature of the place was polka bands that performed every Friday and Saturday night. In 1965, Ray opened a chicken restaurant next door despite the other three chicken places nearby.

Chicken Annie's of Girard was established in 1971. The daughter of Annie Pritcher purchased the Sunflower Tavern and Chicken Dinners on Highway 47 near Girard. Louella was Annie's daughter, and her husband was the son of Mary Pistonick, the original owner of the Sunflower.

Chicken Annie's Pittsburg was opened by Annie's grandson, who is married to Chicken Mary's granddaughter.

The Travel Channel featured Chicken Mary's and Chicken Annie's on the show *Food Wars*.

JEFF DUREE—BANK ROBBER

If there is a man whose life should have been in the movies, it would be Jeff Duree. Fiction cannot beat the real thing many times, and it does not take a big imagination to write a story after the life that Jeff lived. Jeff was a bank robber or, better said, a burglar. By his own admission, he stole over $1 million in his career. His career also takes a path similar to that of Jesse James. As to the specific robberies, it is not actually known because he was blamed for robberies even when he was nowhere near the scene when they happened—such as in the warden's office at Lansing Prison asking to visit his brother.

The myriad newspaper articles do not help much in untangling his story. At one time, he was reported "shot dead" by the Associated Press, yet he died in Lansing Prison in 1961—another case of "reports of my death are greatly exaggerated." And his life was not hard to exaggerate.

Born in Bartlesville, Oklahoma, on July 22, 1893, he was the son of Miles and Margaret Duree and one of thirteen children. His first arrest was through politics. Jeff and his brother Dan were in the dairy business at Bartlesville, and he was doing some landscape work on the side. In the election of 1912, he had worked for the election of the losing candidate for sheriff. This gave rise to a grudge on the part of the winner, and Jeff claimed that he was hounded until he was convicted of larceny and was sent to jail for one year and a day at Granite, Oklahoma. The charge rose from helping his brother

Dan—who was a deputy sheriff by this time—to put out a drunk from the park that he ran. The drunk swore that he was robbed in the process. This charge Jeff maintained was a lie.

When he got out of jail, he claimed to have been hounded continuously, so he moved to Sapulpa, Oklahoma, where he worked as a night clerk at a hotel. His reputation followed him, so he quit that job and bought a pool hall in Daugherty, Oklahoma. Business was not good, and he soon was broke. He married in 1920 and moved back to Sapulpa. He was arrested three times that year and was kept broke by hiring lawyers. He was arrested for a bank robbery in Colorado, and it cost $800 to defend himself from that charge. Soon a bank at Anadarko was robbed, and he was blamed for that also. Jeff had been talking to a sheriff deputy at the hour that the robbery occurred, and he had to get the deputy to provide his alibi. All the attention was starting to hurt the hotel he was working at, and he quit.

Being broke and getting madder and madder at the false accusations, he decided that he might as well make his living burglarizing banks. He robbed a bank in Nebraska successfully and was accused of robbing a train at Edmund, Oklahoma. He decided it was smarter to admit to the bank robbery that he had done than to face the stiffer charges of robbing the train. So he went back to Nebraska and faced the charges of what he really had done.

He did not remember the name of the town where he pulled the bank heist, and that gave some difficulty as to claiming his innocence on the Edmund train robbery. In spite of this, Jeff, his brother Dan and two others were convicted of the train robbery. Evidence was given by a supposed member of the group who turned state's evidence. Jeff was in prison for twenty-nine months before he was permitted to make bond. His ultimate bond was made by an oil man who was a friend of his in Sapulpa.

Jeff's connection to Kansas was his wife's farm outside of Grenola, Kansas. He went back to Lansing Prison and called for permission from the warden to visit his brother; he got permission and went up there. At the same time he was in Lansing, a bank was robbed in Bristow, Oklahoma, by three masked men. Three officers of the bank identified one of them as Jeff even though he was not even in the state. Not knowing that any of this had happened, he took the train to Sapulpa, and as he got off the train, people were staring at him. He passed a policeman who stared at him. He went to the sheriff's office, and the deputy stared at him wide mouthed also. The deputy threw his hands up, frightened, asking him, "What are you doing here?" Jeff still did not know what was going on. Then he was told that he had been identified as one doing the Bristow robbery.

Jeff was outraged, and borrowing a car, he drove straight to the county attorney's office. He explained his situation and told the man to call the warden, Tom Wallace, and get an explanation of where he was and when. The county attorney promised to call off the officers but needed to take Jeff in, and at that, Jeff refused. The man went for his gun, and Jeff beat him to the draw. Jeff told him that he could walk across the street with him and then come back for his gun, which he put in his drawer. He walked with Jeff.

Jeff went to the farm near Grenola where his brother-in-law lived. When he got there, he had just missed seeing a big mess of fish that had been caught. There were lines set in the creek, and he went down to run them. It soon became the wildest experience in his life. They fried up the fish and were finishing when a volley of shots rang out. They had been surrounded by a posse of some sixty men. One man was hit in the eye, with the bullet exiting his head and killing him instantly. Another man was also hit.

Jeff ran away and was sitting behind a tree when the firing at him began again. They were shooting blind, and as Jeff was trying to see who was doing the shooting, a man stood up and aimed a 30-30 at him. Jeff shot at him, and the man's hat flew off. Thinking the man was dead, Jeff ran. As he was running, a voice called out for him to halt. It was Buckles, the sheriff from Sedan, Kansas. Jeff had no intention of stopping, and the sheriff was not going to shoot him in the back. Jeff always carried a deputy's badge in his pocket, and through a series of adventures by taking several cars, he got away. One time, he ran over a cliff and commandeered another car. The adventures of the getaway are not complete as to the surrounding of an area around the river and the manhunt for him. The story was reported in the papers all over the nation.

He commandeered an officer's car and drove it out of town and ditched it, knowing he would not get away with it, but it threw them all off as to where he was. He caught a ride to Bartlesville and was left off two blocks from his sister's place. His family was getting ready to go to his funeral. The man killed in the ambush had been identified as him. He hid out there for three weeks, even with a deputy living across the street.

He went to Radium Springs for the baths at the springs and sent for his wife to come join him; she was tubercular and was dying and had severe rheumatoid arthritis. He could not pay for the treatments, so he decided to pull some jobs. He proceeded to take safes from banks in Arkansas, Kansas, Nebraska, Texas and Oklahoma. He would take a car and take the trunk and install a winch and would winch a safe up into the car and go out in the country and crack the safe in an old barn or under a tent. Jeff's hallmark was that he pulled nighttime jobs, never daylight ones, and he never killed anyone. He kept rough track and knew he had taken over $1 million. He was quiet and consistent and always chose a car with a lot of power. Many times, he and his men would be camped in full view of the highway as they cracked the safe.

He went to hide out in Arizona, and a friend tipped off the officials out there. The sheriff of Maricopa County arrested Jeff, who was then going by the name of Jim Wilson. He was living on a farm near Phoenix, as the climate was better for his wife. All the neighbors were surprised to learn his identity.

He was brought back to Kansas, and several people were convicted of assisting him, including the oilman who was accused of being a fence for him. Some lawmen rated Jeff as the same caliber as Henry Starr. The number of actual crimes he did commit has never been verified. He was put in the Kansas State Penitentiary at Lansing, and on June 7, 1961, he died of a stroke. His grave is unmarked, bearing only a number. Six plots down are the graves of Perry Smith and Richard Hickok, the murderers of the Clutter family at Holcomb. Jeff was described as a very quiet and pleasant fellow.

MAUD STEVENS WAGNER—TATTOO ARTIST

In Lyon County, near Emporia, Maud Stevens was born to David Van Buren Stevens and Elizabeth Vance Stevens around February 12, 1877. Maud's father, David, was a Civil War veteran serving with the 119th Iowa Infantry. David met and married Sarah Jane McGee from Ohio at Toledo, Tamon County, Iowa. The couple ended up living and farming in Lyon County near Emporia, coming to the area between 1865 and 1870. The family moved near Clements in Chase County around 1896. The family story was overshadowed by their one daughter Maud, who went on to be a pioneer of a different type. There is no information on how Maud entered her profession and no insight as to her parents' thoughts about the profession she had chosen. It can be assumed that the family was not very happy about Maud's choice to join the circus. There is one report that the family kept a room for Maud on the other end of the house and contact was limited. It is pointed out that the tattoo on her upper right arm is a tribute to her dad and his military service.

Maud went into the life of the carnival. She became an aerialist and contortionist and worked for many circuses. While she was with the circus,

Maud Stevens Wagner, postcard. *Author's collection.*

she met Gus Wagner, a tattoo artist, at the Louisiana Purchase Exposition (1904 World's Fair). Gus traveled with circuses and sideshows and was billed as the "most artistically marked up man in America." Having gone on a date, Gus gave Maud a lesson in the art of tattooing, and several years later, they were married.

Gus traveled the circus and entertainment circuits for forty-one years. He had shipped out as a seaman and claimed to have learned his tattoo art from natives in Borneo and other islands in the South Pacific. Being a showman all his life, Gus claimed to have 264 tattoos on his body. Born in Marietta, Ohio, a boat building town on the Ohio River, he was inspired by the first tattooed man he saw at age twelve. Captain Costentenous "The Greek" Albanian was in a traveling show, which had a profound effect on the young Gus. Gus got to know the ports of Vera Cruz, London, Capetown, Sydney, Auckland, Honolulu, New York, San Francisco and many others.

Maud became an apprentice, learning the art of tattooing from Gus. It was the traditional hand-poked method of tattooing; this was prior to the invention of the tattoo machine. Maud broke ground becoming one of the most decorated women in the world. After leaving the circus, she and Gus traveled around the United States working as tattoo artists and "tattooing attractions" in vaudeville houses, county fairs and arcades. The couple is credited with bringing tattoo artistry inland from the coastal cities and towns where the practice started.

The couple had two children. Their first daughter, Sarah, died in infancy. Their second daughter, Lotteva Wagner Davis, also became a tattoo artist, although she did not have the art applied to her own body. Although tattooed people were a staple of the circus and sideshow circuit, the actual sighting of more than an ankle on a woman was considered a great scandal. Maud paved the way for women to take a place next to men in the profession.

Maud and Gus would come back to the farm when not on the road and eventually inherited the farm. Gus was hit by lightning in Oklahoma one year prior to his death in 1941. His obituary states that he never recovered from the lightning strike, eventually dying at home near Clements, Kansas.

Maud retired to the farm after Gus's death and died in Oklahoma at her daughter's home in Lawton on January 30, 1961. Maud and Gus are buried with her family in the Homestead Cemetery in Chase County, Kansas.

In 2016, a tattoo company was opened in Emporia carrying the name of the local legend: Maud's Tattoo Company.

MRS. AMY LOUCKS—LAKIN

Maybe it would be better to say Dr. Amy Loucks. Amy M. Sturdtevant was living in Springsboro, Pennsylvania, when she married William P. Loucks. Amy's father, William Sturdtevant, was a carpenter and builder of French ancestry. She was born on August 20, 1843, and was raised in western Pennsylvania. She graduated from high school and began teaching in the public schools in the area.

She had an association with a brother who was a physician and became interested in medicine and surgery. She seriously studied the subjects. In one reference to Amy, she was addressed as "Doctor Amy." Whether she had any formal education in medicine is not recorded, but she had a large amount of practical and hands-on experience throughout her life.

In a narrative about Amy by a brother-in-law, C.A. Loucks, she is described this way: "Probably no woman in the history of the pioneers of western Kansas has contributed more to the welfare and happiness of humanity during that period than Amy M. Loucks." And her record is impressive. When the Loucks moved to western Kansas in the Lakin area, there were no schools, churches or organized society. Kearny County was cow country. The railroad came through, but the nearest doctor was in Dodge City—seventy-five miles away. The town of Lakin was on the railroad and consisted of a depot, eating house, railroad agent's house, store and saloon.

Amy came into town to assess if there were enough children for a subscription school and started the first school in the area. She was active in the growth of the community but was called on frequently to act as doctor and nurse. Some examples of her work: a man had been scalped by Indians but was not dead and the scalp hung over his face. She sewed the scalp back on with fiddle string and a common needle. He was sent back home to his family, where he lived, but he never recovered his sanity from the attack.

Another time, the engineer of the train telegraphed Amy to meet the train on its arrival in Lakin. A woman was giving birth and did not make it any farther than a freight truck on the platform, where Amy assisted in delivering the baby. A train wreck near Lakin had several employees and passengers killed and injured. Amy administered first aid to "a score or more" until a special train from Dodge City with the railroad doctor could arrive with aid. For this work, the railroad gave Amy a lifetime pass.

A posse summoned Amy to treat a badly wounded prisoner. With a vial of carbolic acid as an antiseptic and a knitting needle as a probe, she extracted a bullet with a common set of pincers, saving the man's life. She would nurse the sick and give comfort to the dying and families. As a result, while nursing a patient with a deadly disease, she contracted the disease and died on March 12, 1905.

Amy Loucks had a daughter, Fay A., who lived from 1867 to 1886 and a son, Charles, who lived from 1873 until 1960. Amy is buried in the Lakin Cemetery.

Though not well known by historians, Amy Loucks was one of the pioneers who made living in Kansas better for all who came after her.

OCTAGONAL CITY

Over the years, there have been many attempts to create utopian communities, and there has been a 100 percent failure rate. That pattern holds true in Kansas history. One of the attempts at a perfect society was Octagonal City, a true vegetarian colony, located in Allen County about six miles south of Humboldt. The original plan was to build the colony on the south side of the Neosho River. The project was to be a profitable investment, and the original investors decided that a non-vegetarian moral community was a better investment. So the vegetarian community was built on the north side of the river.

Henry Clubb was the prominent vegetarian in the country and planned the sustainable community with original investors Charles DeWolfe and John McLaurin. Members of the community were under oath to educate their children and uphold a moral lifestyle. The vegetarian philosophy held that the consumption of meat was evil and that the public was backsliding by the consumption of meat, fowl, eggs and dairy products. Clubb's plan was to establish a vegetarian colony in the very center of the country where the faithful would gather to live "in wonderful health and harmony." Clubb published his prospectus in the *Water Cure Journal*.

One of the proponents of the colony was a Quaker who had arrived in the Kansas Territory when his father was appointed superintendent of the Friends Shawnee Mission in Johnson County. John Milton Hadley journeyed around the area and was involved in the Free State movement. Hadley had adopted the vegetarian philosophy, and his antislavery attitude made him a candidate for participation in such a venture. He was idealistic, in support of free labor and free soil. Hadley also was involved with such diverse subjects as phrenology, alchemy, hydropathy and vegetarianism. Although a supporter, he was never well enough to become a settler.

The "dream colony" called Octagonal City was to be settled by members of the Vegetarian Emigration Company. Hadley was never able to join the colony because his health deteriorated, and he had to revert to a meat-eating diet to recover. The city's design was inspired by a scientific idea suggested by the famous phrenologist Orson Squire Fowler. The octagons were considered the most practical design for homes because they permitted the most amount of light to enter.

Henry Clubb imagined eight roads would lead away from the center octagonal town square. From there, the city would be made up of four octagonal villages, complete with octagonal farmhouses, barns, town squares and public buildings. Sixty families ended up living in Octagonal City but found only a windowless log building at the site. The local spring dried up, so there was a lack of water. Then there were the mosquitoes and disease. It had been (incorrectly) promised that a sawmill and gristmill would be at the site. Malnutrition, exhaustion and malaria discouraged the settlers. There were also threats from Indians, border ruffians, crop theft and weather.

Of the one hundred original settlers who first came to the town site in 1856, there were only four left by 1857. These reported more illness as the weather warmed again. The area was remote, and with the railroad arriving, the town of Chanute sprang up just four miles south of Octagonal City. The only thing that remains of the community is the name of Vegetarian Creek.

WALTERSCHEID BROTHERS FOUNDRY— AUTOMOBILE COMPANY

Charles Walterscheid and his family owned a large grain elevator and a large agricultural machinery and supply company in Halbur, Iowa. He was also a shareholder in the First National Bank. His father became ill and needed a change in climate, so Charles took over the family business on his own. Then came a new opportunity in Wichita, Kansas. Charles and his brother Wilhelm took over the B&C Pump Company in Wichita and renamed it Walterscheid Brothers Foundry.

The company was supervised by brother Wilhelm and run by Alexander Glass. The company made items from pumps, windmills, farm equipment, galvanized steel and wood tanks, pipe fittings, belting, hose and boiler work. The list of things built is exhaustive; anything made from aluminum, brass and steel was produced at the Wichita facility. The business was so good that a new large factory was built. Right at the turn of the century, the big rage was automobiles. The brothers sent Glass back east to study the manufacturing techniques of automobile producers. The brothers had a plan, and the design for the creation of a steam-driven automobile was undertaken. This was during the same time that the Cloughley steam auto was being designed and built in Parsons.

The competition for the manufacturing of automobiles caught the attention of a local newspaper. This was a time in Wichita when the bug to become a center of tractor and automobile manufacturing was exciting the town. Two other companies decided to build automobiles also. The Hess & DeLong partnership owned a bicycle shop, and the second floor was turned into a car automobile factory. Also, the Farries started to build an auto.

There was a much-heralded race planned between the three autos. A rally was held in Riverside Park, but results of the race have not been found. A newspaper article showing Glass driving the Walterscheid Steamer to Pratt was published in the local papers. The steamer made the trip and back with

Walterscheid automobile pictured at home with family. *Courtesy of Robert Walterscheid and Walterscheid Productions.*

Circa 1903 Walterscheid Bros., Manufacturers & jobbers of Steam Engine Automobiles and Suppplies, Iron pump machine, and foundry work done to order. 116 - 126 N. Mead. Now employs 43 expert mechanics & occupy a building 107' x 151', most of which is two story. Manufacturers of "Alta", "Wichita", and Peerless Windmills.

Walterscheid Brothers Factory and workers. *Courtesy of Robert Walterscheid and Walterscheid Productions.*

no breakdowns in one of the first promotional events that gave steam to the road improvement movement that would take place over the next few years.

Walterscheid Automobile Company only lasted for two years—1902 and 1903. Only one model is mentioned being produced, but the local pioneer businessman Fritz Schnittzler ordered one of the Walterscheid automobiles be built for him. As of this writing, it is not known if there are any Walterscheids still out there or if there is a collector somewhere that has one. At the time, the factory reported a production rate of six autos per day. It is likely that the conditions that allowed the Cloughley to fail were the same for the Walterscheid—transportation and material difficulties.

The company name of the foundry that the brothers owned eventually was changed to the Wichita Supply Company. In 1916, a fire burned a large portion of the factory. Charles was injured when he fell through a hole in the floor after the fire. There were three other companies sharing space in the building by this time.

Charles Walterscheid died on April 20, 1928, and is buried in Calvary Cemetery in Wichita. Very little has been found on the other two automobile companies. It is noted that the Farries and Hess & DeLong automobiles faded into history, and Wichita never became a center of the automobile manufacturing industry. It would be a few years before the Jones automobile was built in Wichita.

SAM AND ESTHER ZELMAN

The Jewish community in Wichita—and, in fact, the entire state—goes back to the beginning of the territory. With the immigration of Jewish settlers to Kansas, it was the cities like Wichita that established thriving communities that, in spite of achieving simple survival, faced outright hatred and discrimination. The rise of the Ku Klux Klan made life hard not only for the Black community but for the Jewish and Catholic communities as well.

Many Jewish names in the Wichita area are still familiar, and the struggle that the community as a whole had to endure to achieve success is a fascinating story. The Zelman family had such a story of difficulty and success, and much of it was not even well known or discussed in the newspapers until the 1970s.

Sam Zelman was born in Czechoslovakia and immigrated to the United States with the intention of bringing his family over when he was established. He came to the Wichita area and started a clothing store at 602 East Douglas. Fate took a turn for the bad when the Nazis came into power. Most of Sam's families were interned in concentration camps, with the majority not surviving the war. But his oldest daughter did survive, and hers is also a fascinating story.

Esther Zelman somehow managed to survive both Auschwitz and Buchenwald. As the U.S. Army was liberating the camps, she started to yell out the word "Wichita!" hoping that there would be a GI from Kansas who would recognize that she had ties to Wichita. In the troops, there was a Harold Cochran from Wichita. He notified Sam that his daughter had survived the war. At the word of this, Sam broke down in tears of joy.

The actions needed for Esther to be permitted to immigrate to Wichita were started. Waiting in a displaced persons' camp, she became acquainted with Herbert Moses. Herbert had grown up in Germany and had unsuccessfully attempted to flee the Nazis by going to Belgium and then France. Herbert came to New York City. He kept in contact with Esther by mail and came to Wichita for a short visit. During the visit, he married Esther and never went back to New York.

Herbert and Esther joined her father, Sam, in the clothing store, taking it over when Sam died on April 29, 1974. Herbert died in 1991, and Esther ran the shop until 2006. Herbert and Esther were among a very few Holocaust survivors in Kansas. Another was Michael Pinchuk, a Pole who had escaped a Nazi work camp only to be captured by the Soviets and sent to Siberia. At the end of the war, he was released and sent back to Poland. He then immigrated to the United States. Another survivor was Bernard Novick, another native of Poland, who became owner of Novick Iron and Metal.

A group of ten survivors attended an official Yom Ha Shoah commemoration, the presence of which was a reminder to everyone of the horrors of the Nazi death camps. It was only in the 1970s, when this took place, that the local newspaper reported on their stories, when the individuals were in their later years.

The Zelman Building has been converted to the Zelman Lofts. The upper floor was a hotel at one time. Now the building features six studio apartments and one-bedroom upscale apartments.

When Sam's obituary was printed, it listed a son, Charles, who had apparently survived but was unable to immigrate, as he is listed in the USSR. Also listed later is an obituary for Hilda Lindenbaum (Zelman) of Fulton County, Georgia. She is listed as a sister of both Sam and Charles (demonstrating the inconsistency of available information), and she is buried in Wichita.

Sam resided at 422 South Vasser. The story of the Zelmans is not well known in the annals of Kansas history, but it is an important story in demonstrating the resilience of the Jewish community here.

SMITTY THE JUMPER

One of Kansas's true characters was born in Salisbury, North Carolina, before the Wright brothers took to the skies. Smitty the Jumper, as he was known (aka H. Truesdell Smith, Dare Devil Smitty and Tree Top Smitty), grew up along with aviation and was a parachutist in the 1920s and 1930s.

He developed the urge to parachute when many jumpers were being killed on their first (and last) tries. He made a parachute of cheap silk or cotton; some say it was made from JC Penney bedsheets. In 1928, he jumped from an airplane piloted by Andy Burke near Wichita Falls, Texas. He made jumps at air shows, borrowing gear as he could, and finally was given an old parachute with hemp lines. He fashioned additional rigging with a harness from leather and a Model A steering wheel (some say it was a Model T wheel), which he used to crudely steer the chute. He made over two hundred unassisted jumps in his life, and the rest were in tandem.

His original career was as a sign painter. He barnstormed throughout Kansas, Oklahoma, Texas and Arkansas, performing jumps, cutaway jumps (where he would release his chute to fall some more and pull another chute) and wing walking. He found that his pay was higher when his chute deployed lower, and that is how he got the added name "Tree Top Smitty." In 1937, at age forty, his second wife persuaded him to give up jumping since she was raising his three children. Sign painting paid better and was safer. He would create signs as large as two-story buildings and on aircraft noses. He painted a bird logo emblem for the TV show *Sky King*'s Songbirds. He also became a dance instructor, something he claimed he had been doing since the 1920s.

In the late 1960s, he returned to the air show circuit. His later jumping career was marked with accidents and near misses, but he survived them all. In 1960, at age sixty-one, he made a jump at the National Air Show at Wichita, Kansas, jumping from U.L. "Rip" Gooch's airplane. As he went out the door, he blacked out, but he woke up in time to open his chute at tree-top level. In 1972, at age seventy-four, he broke his leg near Maize trying to land next to a group of girls. The girls carried him to the drop zone, and he partied all night with them and did not go to the hospital until the next day.

In 1974, at age seventy-five, he jumped near Lincoln, Nebraska, and blacked out again, waking up in time to see that he was headed for a black water pond at the city dump. He steered clear but hit the dike and busted his leg, hip and pelvis. This was jump 211 and his last solo. He ended up in a full-body cast for two and a half months.

In 1981, he was invited to be on the *Tonight Show with Johnny Carson* and was billed as the world's oldest skydiver. At age eighty-seven, in 1985, he attached himself to skydiver Mark McCafferty near El Dorado, Kansas, making his 216th jump. In 1985, before a crowd of two hundred thousand at the EAA National Meet in Oshkosh, Wisconsin, he made another tandem jump. On December 15, 1985, at age eighty-eight and jump number 216, he tandem jumped at Perris Valley, California, extending his title of World's Oldest Skydiver with his son Jerry Smith, age listed at fifty-two or fifty-four. This put Smitty in the record books for the oldest father/son jump. Jerry had made his first jump the day before. In 1985, Smitty jumped as a tandem with the Mirror Image World Championship Team sponsored by Coors Light.

Over a five-year period, he made fifteen tandem jumps. On July 5, 1990, at age ninety-one in Albert Lea, Minnesota, he made jump number 221, his last.

Smitty died on June 7, 1995, in a nursing home in Wichita. He had accomplished jumping in every decade until his death and left a legacy of derring-do. Very few remember the man who defied age and danger and entertained Johnny Carson.

UNIVERSITY FARM

So if you want to go to university to get an education in agriculture, you go to K-State, right? Not necessarily. Many people do not know this, but the University of Kansas also has a farm and offers agricultural degrees as well as environmental studies. The original farm belonged to the first governor of the state of Kansas, James Robinson. The farm was given to the University of Kansas by his widow in 1911.

The farm consists of three thousand acres and has an education center with classrooms. There are studies in native plant communities, land management, water quality issues, native medicinal plant research, algae fuel (bio diesel) research and public sanitation research for third-world countries, including Bolivia. The farm is part of the National Ecological Observatory Network (NEON), which is a continent-wide monitoring project.

The Department of Food and Agriculture at the University of Kansas offered this description: "There is lots of interest in and debate about food and agriculture in our contemporary culture. This is evident by recent food crises, the evolution of Foodidom, the popularity of cooking shows, growing alternative agricultural production and consumer movements, and the popularity of documentaries like *Food Inc*. This pathway is designed to engage students in these timely and important issues and to guide them toward finding food and agriculture-related courses from especially the humanities and social sciences."

The KU farm also includes the University of Kansas Student Farm. The farm got its start in a 2009 Environmental Studies Capstone Course where a group of students drew up plans for a place where people could grow their own food. Participation in the farm is open to KU students, faculty and staff. The farm experienced rapid growth in the first five years. The student farm maintains a Facebook page, website and e-mail address. The student farm also supports and works with community gardens in the Lawrence community. Each student can apply for a garden pit and can make proposals for projects.

So if you would like to have a BA in agriculture rather than a BS degree, the KU program may be for you. The farm has been a subject story on *Sunflower Journey* and in other publications. The farm is part of the Environmental Studies Program in the College of Liberal Arts and Sciences.

RALPH WINSHIP—MAJESTIC THEATER

Ralph Winship was the owner of the oldest theater in the state. His father, Fred Winship, came to the Phillipsburg community from Kearney, Nebraska. Fred spent his first night in the attic of a farm store on the northwest corner of the town square. He worked by day and then opened a store in a twenty-five-foot frame building on the southeast corner of the square where the Majestic Theater now stands.

Ralph's family was in the mercantile business, and he had begun working at an early age in the family business. Ralph's father decided to add a second story to the business building and use most of it as an opera house. The upstairs was described as "magnificent" and had Venetian red walls trimmed in gold. Half of the building was owned by the Masonic Lodge and was destroyed by fire. The original building was restored and still stands today.

The opera house had road companies that came through, and the first box office was on the second floor of the seven-hundred-seat theater. Some of the performers were the Wilkes Musical Players, which had twenty members, mostly girls, along with special scenery. The Weldon Comedy Company and the Golden Meads Metropolitan Girls were other acts. The largest company to play at the theater was a minstrel show of thirty-five people who brought their own band and orchestra and arrived by chartered train. Admission was $1.25, which was a high price for the time.

The bricks for the building were manufactured right there in the local brick factory. By this time, Thomas Edison's White Magic was becoming popular. The films had no story or plot, and still pictures were used in a lot of projections on the screen. A year or two after opening the theater, Ralph's father went out of the mercantile business and rented the building to a promoter who showed motion pictures. Electric lights had been installed in Philipsburg, and the promoter was an ambitious employee of the electric company. He was a bit overly ambitious and soon was behind on the rent. Fred quickly was fed up and asked Ralph to take over the business. Fred believed that movies were the coming thing, but Ralph had no desire to get into the business. By carefully watching the bottom line, the movies soon became a thriving business. Children cost a nickel and adults a dime to get in. The popularity of the theater began to grow steadily. Other operators of movie theaters gradually shut down because they did not want to remodel or upgrade their buildings. The Majestic would bring in more and more expensive films. By the 1920s, it was obvious that the traveling road shows were doomed, and the opera house was closed. The ground floor was remodeled, and a big screen was installed.

In 1927, the first talking picture came to town. The sound was on phonographic records, which were supposed to be synchronized with the film. Problems were frequent. The film was brittle and would break, and when making the repairs, the soundtrack would get off a little bit more. Prices at that time were up a dime for children and a quarter for adults. Stars such as Mary Pickford, Douglas Fairbanks, Buck Jones, Tom Mix and Clara Bow were featured in the shows. Ralph had an alphabetical file for every show and short subject that ran at the Majestic back to 1926. The toughest days were in the 1930s during the Depression. The theater concentrated on motion pictures, and the admission was raised to thirty-five cents for adults. As an added incentive, one night a week was called Bank Night. A twenty-five-dollar drawing was held each week, and if the winner was not there, the money would be added to the jackpot for the following week. There were overflowing crowds on those nights.

Following the Depression, the theater prospered until television started to cut into entertainment time for people. Rising costs and declining attendance, as well as declining population in the rural areas, were being felt. Back in the

1920s, Ralph started an open-air theater to beat the summer heat. He set up a tent on the lot just east of the theater. Seating was on planks, but this did not last long due to wind, rain, dust and mosquitoes. Ralph could not tolerate people who tried to sneak into the shows, but his wife did not help out much there. Belle felt sorry and let a lot of freeloaders in. Son-in-law D.T. "Bud" Brown built a drive-in movie on the edge of town in the 1950s. Ralph retired after running the theater for sixty-three years. The drive-in was sold to Mr. and Mrs. Sterling Bagby of nearby Stockton.

Ralph was born on July 26, 1883, and died on September 14, 1969. The building was sold to new owners who ran it until 2000. A group of local volunteers purchased the building for one dollar. The building has been renovated, and more plans are in the works. It is run by volunteers. The Majestic is the oldest operating theater in the state.

NEOSHO FALLS

A traveling writer who posts blogs came into Neosho Falls and called it a ghost town—which was news to the residents who live there. The 2010 census put the population at 141, and it is smaller now. There are people still living there, keeping a quiet way of life. Although there are a lot of abandoned buildings and piles of rubble, there is still civic pride in Neosho Falls. The origins of the town had great promise, and for a time, the county seat was here. There were 1,200 residents at its peak. There were mills on the river and a lot of business.

Located on the Neosho River, the town was platted by a town company led by Benjamin F. Goss and his brother N.S. Goss. One of the first works of the town was to build a dam across the river. A mill and later a powerhouse were built there. The dams and buildings are still there. In 1873, a second mill was built—a woolen mill.

The only residents in the area prior to the founding of the town were Judge John Woodman and John Chapman. At the time, the area was the reserve of the New York Indian tribe. The area was not open for settlement, but this did not stop the settlers from coming. The New York Indians never settled there and refused to; they had a small settlement near Fort Scott. In 1860, the area was opened for settlement.

The first teacher in the area was E.H. Curtis, who would later become a colonel of a Black regiment in the Civil War. In 1867, a vote was taken, and

Neosho Falls Mill and Dam. *Courtesy of the Kansas Sampler Foundation.*

Neosho Falls became the county seat. Another vote was taken since the town of Chellis disputed the claim. The county seat dispute would continue for the next eight years, finally leaving Neosho Falls out in the cold and Yates Center the victor.

The first newspaper was the *Frontier Democrat* in 1869 by Isaac Boyle. In 1870, it was sold to William Slavens, and the name changed to the *Neosho Falls Advertiser*. The newspaper changed hands several times and became the *Woodson County Post* in 1873.

The Union Pacific Railroad came through in 1870, later becoming the Missouri, Kansas and Texas Railroad. Later, the Atchison, Topeka and Santa Fe Railroad came through, making the town a major transportation center.

A major enterprise was the Neosho Valley Fair, which took in four counties—Allen, Anderson, Greenwood and Woodson. The fair was very successful and was known far and wide. In 1879, the fair was host to guests President Rutherford B. Hayes and his wife, General William T. Sherman and several state guests.

The town started to dwindle when electricity replaced water power in the 1920s. It was hit with a major flood in 1926, killing one and doing thousands of dollars in damage. Both railroads eventually left, and the Depression hit the town hard. Oil gave a little boost to the economy for a while. The newspaper shut down in 1935. Another huge flood hit in 1951 and devastated a large area and prompted the construction of several reservoirs in the state. The high school shut down in 1961 and the grade school in 1969.

Today, there are no businesses left in Neosho Falls. There is a fire station and community center and also many houses that are well maintained. It is a surprise to those living there that the town was pronounced a "ghost town" by a visitor.

KANSAS HIGHWAY PATROL

Have you ever wondered about the beginnings of the troopers that you see patrolling the highways of Kansas? We hear now about how the highways developed and the development of the automobile. The state did not have any law enforcement agencies in the early days. The functions of the United States marshals and the local jurisdictions left a lot of loopholes in pursuit of the bad guys. Jurisdictions for town marshals, township constables or police officers ended at their boundaries. The sheriff was in charge of county law and serving state warrants from the district courts. U.S. marshals were responsible for violations of federal matters. There could be cooperation between agencies, but in many cases the politics of the area would have the agencies pulling away from each other.

In the 1920s and 1930s, there was a rash of bank robberies and other crime sprees. The Volstead Act implementing Prohibition would bring a whole new level of money and corruption to the country. The Midwest was crisscrossed by criminals such as John Dillinger, Baby Face Nelson and Bonnie and Clyde. With new levels of violence, a proportionate number of officers were killed. Highway building was also in its infancy, and as the miles of pavement shortened the time between points, there was a corresponding number of wrecks and reckless driving.

In 1933, Governor Alfred Landon, the Highway Department attorney and the Kansas legislature moved to create a force of ten motor vehicle inspectors. The creation of this group was the forerunner of the Highway Patrol. The legislature officially authorized the Highway Patrol in 1937. The force was created with a superintendent, assistant superintendent and forty-five troopers. Responsibilities consisted of reducing crashes and enforcing traffic, vehicle and license laws. The first superintendent was Kansas City veteran Jack B. Jenkins.

Troopers were to be a minimum of twenty-four years of age, in good health, of high moral character and have no criminal record. As late as 1945, the force members had to be half of the party of the governor and half of the party of the runner-up in the election. Troopers rode as pairs until the 1960s, at which time each member was assigned a car.

The original fleet of vehicles consisted of four motorcycles and thirty-one automobiles. In 1950, the Highway Patrol started patrolling the Kansas Turnpike and the protective services and driving the governor. In the 1960s, an airplane was added to the patrol. In 1976, the Capital Area Security Patrol, now known as the Capital Police or Troop K, was added. In 1988, the Motor Carriers Inspectors were moved from the Department of Revenue to the patrol.

In 1994, the training academy was moved to the former Marymount College campus in Salina. The first female trooper joined in 1981. Up to this date, the Kansas Highway Patrol has lost ten officers in the line of duty:

Trooper Maurice R. Plummer, December 6, 1944 (auto accident)

Trooper Jimmie D. Jacobs, October 6, 1959 (auto accident)

Trooper John B. McMurray, December 9, 1944 (vehicular assault)

Kansas Highway Patrol cruiser. *Courtesy of the Kansas State Historical Society.*

Lieutenant Bernard C. Hill, May 28, 1967 (auto accident)

Sergeant Eldon K. Miller, October 9, 1968 (gunfire)

Trooper James Donald Thornton, October 2, 1973 (gunfire)

Trooper Conroy G. O'Brian, May 24, 1978 (gunfire)

Trooper Ferdinand Fredrick "Bud" Pribbenow, July 11, 1981 (gunfire)

Master Trooper Larry Leo Huff, November 26, 1993 (auto accident)

Master Trooper Dean Allen Goodheart, September 6, 1995 (struck by vehicle)

The mission continues today, assisting local jurisdictions and the KBI on cases and striving to make the highways and the state a safer place to be.

KANSAS PACK GOATS— DWITE AND MARY SHARP

A pack goat is not something you think about when you hear the word *goat*. There are many things that come to mind, including dairy and mohair, and even tasty meat, but a pack goat? The Sharps live near Council Grove and raise and train pack goats. In fact, the group was one of the main attractions at the first Mother Earth News Fair held in Lawrence in 2013.

The group is known as the All-Wether Marching Band. Of course, the name is a play on words; a wether is a neutered male goat. While displaying the fifteen-member pack train at the fair, the Sharps conducted workshops about using goats to pack into the rough country. Along with this group, the Sharps were invited to bring along two of their mammoth donkeys to the fair.

The Sharps' ranch is known as the Paradise Ranch, and they operate under Paradise Ranch Adventures LLC. The couple takes people into the country, the Flint Hills and around Council Grove to demonstrate the use of the goats as pack animals and to instruct those who would train and use their own goats. Counting the couple's grandkids, there five generations of Sharps living in the Council Grove area. Dwite's great-great-great-grandfather was born near Belfry and was an ox team driver and merchant on the Santa Fe Trail.

Paradise Ranch is located at the original site of the Kaw Indian Reservation. The couple keeps a variety of animals at the ranch, such as chickens, guineas, dogs, mammoth donkeys and seven different breeds of goats. The couple offers an agritourism experience with trail rides, horse-drawn wagon rides, meals and an overnight stay.

The couple and their goats have appeared at many fairs and events around the country and were featured in *Goat Tracks Magazine*. They have participated in field days at the goat research facility at Langston University in Oklahoma. The couple sold several goats to the Ringling Brothers Barnum and Bailey Circus, where they performed tricks.

The interest in pack goats was an outgrowth of the couple's favorite hobby. They enjoyed backpacking in North Carolina and decided that they would enjoy it even more if they had something to carry packs for them. They had heard about John Mionczynski's goats that carried loads over rough terrain during the naturalist study of big horn sheep.

The Sharps developed a breeding program, and they have a large variety of breeds at the ranch. They include American Alpines, Brown Oberhaslis, Toggenburgs, Black Nubians and White Saanans. By selectively breeding, the couple developed their own breed known as the Sabor. This breed combines the Saanans and the South African Boer. Most of their goats weigh between 250 and 300 pounds and can carry 25 to 30 percent of their body weight in aluminum framed packs.

The statistics of animal husbandry in the state of Kansas include many familiar breeds, but the state is the center of raising and training pack goats.

A pack goat posing in the High Country. *Courtesy of Dwite Sharp.*

Left: A pack goat at rest. *Courtesy of Dwite Sharp.*

Below: A family with a pack goat string in a forest. *Courtesy of Dwite Sharp.*

Left: A string of pack goats in a forest. *Courtesy of Dwite Sharp.*

Below: Dwite Sharp with Mudslide at Meadow Lake in Wyoming. *Courtesy of Dwite Sharp.*

Above: A pair of pack goats taking a rest. *Courtesy of Dwite Sharp.*

Right: Dwite Sharp with Geranimo crossing a bridge at Lanston University. *Courtesy of Dwite Sharp.*

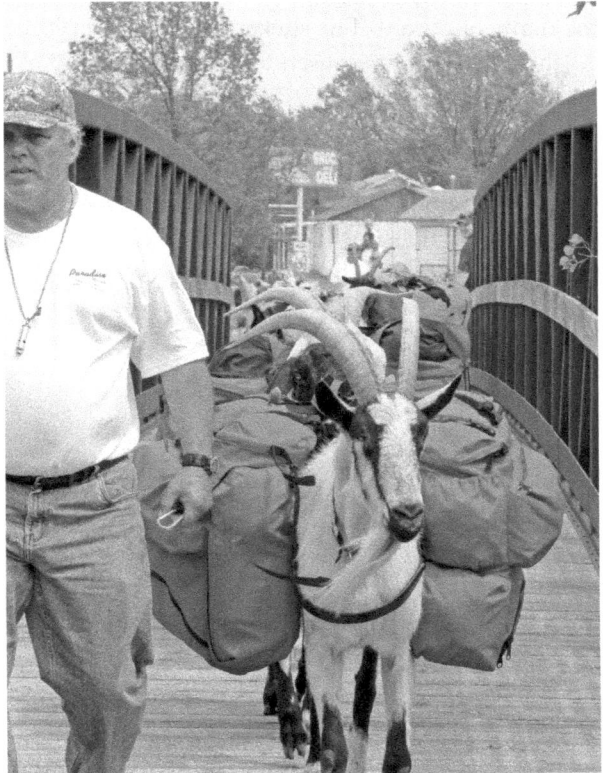

HENRY'S CANDY

The long and the short of it is as you go through Dexter, there is a candy company right on the highway called Henry's Candy Company. It is the home of the original Oh Henry candy bar. Tom Henry was running the Peerless Candy factory in Arkansas City. In 1919, he invented a candy bar that was then called the Tom Henry Bar. He sold the candy bar in 1920 to the Williamson Candy Company of Chicago.

When looking for the Oh Henry bar in Williamson history, the fact that the company acquired the bar from Kansas is conveniently omitted. Williamson changed the name of the candy bar to Oh Henry in 1923. There had been stories of the bar being named after the author O. Henry, but the company put out the story that it was named after a young man named John Goss who worked for the company and announced that he was going to market the bar and make it a national bestseller. Promotion during that time was not as easy as today, and he had stickers made up that said OH HENRY. Since he was given no funds for promotion, this was the least expensive way to put the name out there. The stickers went on everything, including automobiles. As the curiosity was roused as to what it meant, the candy bar took off and became a bestseller.

Another story about naming the candy bar was about an incorrigible young man who worked for the company and made the women always say, "Oh, Henry." That was another great marketing ploy that comes from the company that it was sold to, the Nestle Company; it was distributed in Canada by Hershey. The real story gets lost.

Henry's Candy 2. *Courtesy of Barry and Victoria Ward.*

Tom Henry went to Arkansas and opened up a candy store in Little Rock. His son Patrick came to Dexter, Kansas, and opened a candy company on Main Street. As a youth, the author remembers going into the old store downtown and the big copper kettles and big stone slab tables that the hot candy was poured on. They made the treat of the day there. My favorite was the caramels.

Later on, a new building was built on the highway, and Patrick's daughter and family ran the candy factory and store. Some of the same equipment is still being used from the original store. Yes, you can get the Oh Henry bar there, but it is called the Momma Henry Bar. The family still uses the original recipes that Tom handed down. The company is open 363 days a year.

If you call ahead, they will be happy to give group tours.

LOYD RATTS—FARMER, INVENTOR, CENTENARIAN

Loyd Ratts was somewhat of a celebrity in the farming community of Ransom in Stafford County. He was a living witness to history and continued to make history as he went along. Loyd started farming when everything was horse drawn and moved through the age of the tractor and mechanized farming until today's no-till, GPS and electronic systems. As he went along the way, he found that if you needed something, you fixed it or built it yourself.

In an interview in the *Kansas Farmer* at age 101, he explained that when he was 4, his father put him on a wagon load of wheat and sent him to town while he loaded another wagon. Loyd was working a four-horse team with a harrow when he was 6. He was 10 when his father purchased a Fordson tractor; he remarked that he did "quite a bit of farming with it."

The family was farming in Stafford County and purchased an aunt's ground to keep them from losing it. Along with the farm and a mortgage came the aunt—who was an invalid—and her son to raise. Then the Depression hit, and it was a struggle to keep from losing everything. The amazing thing was that the family also farmed land in southwest Kansas and used the same equipment. The tractor would be pulled between farms with a Model A Ford, a 185-mile trip. They ended up farming three thousand acres in southwest Kansas and a half section near Ransom.

Loyd Ratts, first customer at the new White's Foodliner in St. John, age 103. Famous farmer, inventor and businessman. *Courtesy of the* Pratt Tribune.

Loyd was able to get a job as a farm mechanic with hours that allowed him to still do the farming. He spent two years building barracks at Camp Funston (1939–40) and worked on twin-engine pilot training planes and on gliders at Cessna Aircraft in Wichita between 1940 and 1942. He returned to the farm to help support the war effort raising crops.

The Ratts families were very conservation minded and were able to grow crops when their neighbors' land was blowing away. Many landowners had the Rattses farm their land so it would not blow away and would be productive. In 1954, Loyd started the Ratts repair shop on the farm, which kept his neighbors' and his own equipment working through the times when money was scarce.

At age 99, Loyd was still active in farming with his son-in-law and grandson. He also invented a simple device that could do a very dangerous job that many farmers get injured or killed doing every year. He invented a way to open and close the lids on grain bins from the ground. He claimed that he could still crawl up on grain bins at age 99, but his family would not be happy about it. At age 101, Loyd was still manufacturing the device and selling it from his farm factory and doing a lot of the work on it himself.

There have been many newspaper articles on Loyd Ratts over the years. When he says he retired, it just meant he slowed down but was still there to help on the farm and in the factory. In fact, *Wichita Eagle* reporter Beccy Tanner from St. John was working on a biography of Loyd at the time of this writing. Beccy is related to Loyd, so the talent does run in the family.

In Loyd's shop, there are over sixty years of artifacts—tools for manufacturing for agriculture that he built and used over the years. He is related to Jesse Shields, another Kansas native and the inventor of the pneumatic tractor tire for Firestone. The testing of the tires was done on relatives' farms in the Ransom area. Loyd learned how to remove the lugs from steel wheels and mount the new tires on the rims for tractors. He commented that if he needed a tool and could not afford to buy one, or if one did not exist, he could just build what he needed. He would spend hours studying and figuring out how to tackle problems and how to make things work.

At 101, Loyd was still working in his shop, moving around workstations in his motorized wheelchair. And he was still teaching others how to do things. Loyd was the first customer in the new White's Foodliner supermarket in St. John. He passed away at age 103 on November 30, 2018.

KARRIN ALLYSON—JAZZ GREAT

Karrin Allyson was born in Great Bend. Her father was a Lutheran minister, and her mother was a psychotherapist, teacher and classical pianist. Karrin grew up in Omaha, Nebraska, and spent her last year of high school in San Francisco. As a young girl, she studied classical piano, sang at her local church, was in musical theater and started writing songs.

Karrin attended the University of Nebraska at Omaha on a classical piano scholarship. She majored in classical piano and minored in French. She became the lead singer for an all-female rock band called Tomboy. She developed an interest in jazz and performed in a jazz swing choir in college, as well as her own jazz ensemble that played at venues around Omaha. She graduated in 1986 and moved to Minneapolis to concentrate on a jazz career. In 1990, she moved to Kansas City, and her career took off.

Karrin's debut album was *I Didn't Know About You*. That album was so well received that it was re-released on Concord Records in 1993. Concord released eight more albums in Kansas City. She moved to New York in 1998 with her longtime partner, Bill McGlaughlin; the two had met in Kansas, and he was a classical music radio host.

From 1992 to 2015, Karrin released sixteen albums and toured the country. In 2015, Karrin went back into the studio with a new agreement with Motema Records for a look at the music of Rodgers and Hammerstein. She would spend two out of three days playing in major festivals, concert venues and clubs in the United States and make tours in Brazil, Japan, Australia and the great cities of Europe. In 2014, she was featured as a vocal soloist at the Newport Folk Festival.

Karrin moves easily through the American songbook from Gershwin and Porter to the great jazz songbook of Duke and Thelonious, Miles, Dizzy, Bonnie Raitt, Joni Mitchell and Jimmy Webb. She has been praised by critics such as Gary Giddens of the *Village Voice* and the *New York Times*.

Karrin has a passion for teaching and does private lessons, masters classes and clinics all over the world. She has a voice described as sweetness with a core of toughness. She is also a great bandleader. She is described as making it sound so effortless that it conceals a deep musical sophistication.

She is doing a lot of writing and as of this story promises an album of all original songs. It is said that she unites the wide world of

Karrin Allyson, jazz great. *Courtesy of Jim O'Keefe.*

music by bringing it together and making sense of it all—high praise for a girl from Great Bend!

DIXIE LEE—MADAM

Being notorious leaves a little bit of a trail, and Dixie Lee is one who was in a profession that is mostly known by police blotters and newspaper accounts. Being a savvy businesswoman is how Dixie had a little public notoriety that we can find out about today. At the time, she was a well-known figure, and a lot was probably known, or invented, about her. This information was not talked about in "polite" society. Yet it was the businesses like Dixie's that paid for the infrastructure of early Wichita. Those who lived on "the hill" were dead set on Wichita becoming the New York of the plains. The early days of the town were built by many businesspeople, but the public facilities were paid for by fines on prostitution, gambling and liquor. Behind this, Dixie ran three of the best houses in town. There were many other bawdyhouses that ran pretty much in the open and were notorious—places like Kelly House, Green Cottage, Silvers House, Black and Tan, Dug Out, Paradise and Little Georgia's. The Red Light was a bit classier and did not seem to have a reputation, as did the Iron Clad. Dixie's house did not have any nickname and was just Dixie Lee's Place. The lower-class houses would let the women be seen in various stages of dress or undress, so anyone going by could not mistake what business they were in. Dixie's girls never showed themselves unless fully dressed and did not bring any notoriety from passersby. With the class and distinction that Dixie had, the clientele was of a better class, so there were never any problems and the place was as much a gentlemen's club and restaurant as a bawdyhouse.

Inez "Dixie Lee" Griffing was born at Table Rock, Pawnee County, Nebraska, on January 13, 1862. Her father was Osymn Griffing and mother Sarah L. Reevis. She had four siblings: Ella G., Anna, Ernest and Jesse. She married Charles A. Oppenhiemer and had a tumultuous marriage. There was a filing for divorce and stories of ups and downs in the relationship, but Charles put an end to it with a bullet in his head. According to another report, Charles was despondent over the divorce and had been arrested in Kansas City. He was supposed to have dissolved two carbolic acid pills in a glass of water and died a horrible death from the effects of the poisoning. The poisoning story seems to be the more credible. This demonstrates how stories are created and perpetuated through time by various sources.

There was one notorious incident regarding Dixie's institution that made the papers when a reporter with the *Wichita Beacon* pursued the story of a blackmail case by a woman named Kittie Paxton of a Senator O'Brian in the amount of $400. Charges were never officially filed, and there was a great song and dance by all parties involved. The reporter complained that witnesses were not talking but somehow confirmed the cashing of a $400 check. The senator, who was not planning to leave town, did so as soon as his business was conducted. The incident did leave a stigma on Dixie, and she soon left her property in charge of some local men and left town. Earlier, Dixie had made the papers over an action that was being taken by the city on Wichita Street, where her houses were located. The city was vacating half of the street in order for the Missouri Pacific to expand its depot. Dixie filed suit along with other property owners for a stay, but the city commission went ahead with the eminent domain action anyway.

At one point while she was still married, Dixie adopted a little girl. An officer with the Humane Society took the child and placed her in a children's home and tried to get the courts to take the child away from Dixie. She was able to get custody and put her with a friend somewhere outside of town. This shook her up, and she made arrangements to go back to Kansas City, where she had learned her trade before coming to Wichita. The girl, named Ruth, had been the daughter of a girl who had not been in the business but ended up pregnant. Dixie adopted Ruth after Ruth's mother died just a couple days after delivery. They are listed in the Kansas City directory in 1894 next to the famous Kansas City madam Annie Chambers. Dixie died in San Francisco after traveling there to visit her family. In declining health, she died on January 13, 1901, at Lane Hospital. She had written her will on January 8, prior to her death. She was thirty-eight years and fifteen days old when she passed. San Francisco records do not exist since the great earthquake and fire of 1906 destroyed the city and all the records. Dixie is buried in Steele Cemetery in Falls City, Nebraska. She left her daughter very well off.

Today, the character is kept alive at Old Cowtown Museum with the Dixie Lee Dance Troop.

NANNIE JONES

Who was Nannie Jones, what did she do and where did she go? A writer for the *Wichita Eagle* did a story in the Neighbors section of March 6, 2016, raising the question after noticing in the Tihen Notes a short description of a news article. Reporter Joe Stumpe was intrigued and decided to investigate the article. The short synopsis in Tihen Notes was about a woman who was denied entrance to Wonderland Park on Ackerman Island because of her color. Reports called her "Negro," and a city listing placed her as "Mulatto"; census records list her with a "c," which stood for colored.

Before 1890, there was no official segregation in Kansas. That changed with the 1896 *Plessy v. Ferguson*, which allowed "separate but equal" public facilities. This was the time when Jim Crow became prevalent across the country. In this timeframe, the Black population was increasing in Wichita. Even though Kansas was a supporter of abolishing slavery and welcomed the Exoduster movement in the state, there was also an increase in the activities of the Ku Klux Klan.

The listing of Nannie's husband, William, ranged from fire department to police detective and real estate agent. The Joneses are listed as living at 906 Water Street in Wichita. This is the area where the Sedgwick County Jail is currently located and near the Kansas African American Museum.

Nannie became a part of history due to the fact that she and a friend had free passes to Wonderland as a result of her husband putting an advertising card in the window of his business. An assistant manager of the park refused the pair entrance because they were Black. As a result, Nannie filed a discrimination suit against the park for its actions. The newspaper account showed Nannie as winning the lawsuit, and she was ordered to receive $400 of the $5,000 that she had sued for.

The fact that she was able to file the suit and get a jury verdict had everything to do with her lawyer. Senator O.A. Bentley represented Nannie. Bentley was a prominent lawyer and politician of the time and the author of the *Wichita and Sedgwick County History* in 1910. Court records cannot be found as to the appeal that was filed by the losing side in the case, and there is no record of if she received the judgment that the court awarded.

Nannie went on to live her life; she died and was buried in the Maple Grove Cemetery in Wichita. This and Highland Park are the two cemeteries where many of the founding and prominent members of early Wichita are buried. The grave was never marked. When the article came out in the *Wichita Eagle*, the reporter had contacted the African American Museum, a professor at WSU who had written a book on Black women and other museums, and nothing was known about Nannie. She is mentioned in a

Nannie Jones's headstone. *Courtesy of Barb Meyers.*

book by author and professor Brent Campney, who wrote the book *This Is Not Dixie: Racist Violence in Kansas, 1861–72*.

What a great story of courage in a time before the fight for civil rights really made any headway! But the name Nannie Jones faded into obscurity and ended with an unmarked grave. The rest of the story is told by Beccy Tanner in the *Wichita Eagle* on July 20, 2016, in an article titled "Righting a Wrong, Wichitans Gather to Honor Nannie Jones." It tells the story of the actions of a lot of people after reading the original story. Money was raised, and today a new headstone marks the graves of Nannie and William.

Nannie was a lady of courage who stood up for what was right. Even though she was forgotten by history, she has now been rediscovered and honored. By the way, Wonderland changed its policy after the court decision. It was only a few years later that the strangest baseball game in Wichita history took place on Ackerman Island when an all-Black team played the Ku Klux Klan baseball team. The park closed, and in the 1950s, Ackerman Island was removed from the river because of flooding.

CROSS MANUFACTURING

One thing for sure is that there is a lot of time to think when you are in the field farming. For centuries, it was hard drudgery, and the power unit was manpower, horsepower or oxenpower. Since the nation was founded, the huge majority of people lived on farms, raised all of their own food and sold the surplus. And all this time, young men dreamed about how to make the work easier, faster and more efficient. That is why a blacksmith named John Deere improved the plow and a man named McCormick invented an easier way to bring in the harvest. For those well-known names, there were thousands that have been lost to history—many successful and many just plain failures. But the dreams never stopped.

Such is the story of James H. Cross and Charles R. Cross. These Kansas men were in the middle of a revolution that was taking place on the farm. With the advent of power farming, there was still a lot of labor involved, and these two saw a way to improve the way things were done. There was a new source of energy that was being pioneered, and it had been utilized in several fashions during the war. It was known as hydraulic power. Using fluid under high pressure was a technology that was applicable in many situations and could do more than just plain sweat labor could accomplish.

Looking at the way implements were put down and raised up, the Cross brothers utilized the technology to produce hydraulic cylinders. The demand for the hydraulic cylinder grew at a staggering pace, and tractor manufacturers increasingly equipped their products with a hydraulic system.

Starting in 1949, the Cross Manufacturing Company started to produce hydraulic cylinders that were used in agriculture and many other applications. The first building dedicated exclusively to the Cross Manufacturing Company was built in Lewis, Kansas. By 1955, the factory had grown to 100,000 square feet and produced 100,000 cylinders a year. In this year, the Pratt Adapter division was acquired. The next year, the company began a new facility in Kinsley.

In 1969, a fire struck the Lewis plant, and it had to be rebuilt. They also began construction on a second cylinder plant in Lamar, Colorado. In 1970, a facility opened in Hays. During the 1970s, the company expanded with locations in Colorado, Mississippi and Puerto Rico and began affiliations in Australia and Mexico. Also in the 1970s, the company started building gear pumps and the SQV sequence valve for row markers.

The year 1982 marked a period of severe farm depression that affected producers and manufacturers that catered to them. The company entered a period when it was in Chapter 11. John H. Cross was appointed president of the company. In 1988, the company emerged from Chapter 11 and was successfully reorganized. By 1990, the standard stock warehouse had been expanded and new environmental safeguards put into place.

The Cross Manufacturing Company in 1995 and 1996 voluntarily repaid in full creditors who had chosen a discount settlement in the Chapter 11 proceedings. The company had received numerous environmental safety awards for its efforts to reduce waste and pollution and maintain a safe working environment for its employees.

The company continues as a leader in the field of hydraulics, and the president, John Cross, credits a great working relationship with its employees and customers as a basis for its success. One other thing that he gives credit to is the dedication to the Lord that the company made during its time of trouble. The company is an asset to Kansas, its employees, its customers and agriculture.

A lot of progress for two farm boys who had a dream.

BUDDY ROGERS—OLATHE

Buddy Rogers was born in Olathe on August 13, 1904. He was the son of a newspaperman and judge. Besides editing the *Olathe Mirror*, his father had been appointed the "marrying judge" for the county. Buddy graduated from Olathe High School. He studied music and played several instruments. He also had a small dance band. He attended the University of Kansas, and before he graduated, he was "discovered" by talent scouts from Paramount Studios in 1925. Buddy's father had encouraged him to enter a talent scout contest.

Buddy Rogers, actor. *Courtesy of the Kansas State Historical Society.*

Buddy found himself in the movie *So's Your Old Man* with W.C. Fields. This movie was filmed in New York. Soon he found himself in California in a budding movie career. He won a starring role in the movie *Wings*. This film was his first to win an Academy Award for Best Picture. It is now considered a classic. In the 1920s and 1930s, Buddy was called "America's Boy Friend."

During World War II, Lieutenant Buddy Rogers served as a flight instructor for the United States Navy.

Buddy was a talented trombone player and fronted bands, but as described in *American Dance Bands on Record and Film, 1915–1942*, "Rogers was not a traditional band leader but a film actor fronting a band for publicity purposes." Buddy had parts in many pictures in the 1920s and 1930s, as well as his band gigs. While in a movie, he caught the eye of Mary Pickford, who was the richest and most popular actress in Hollywood. She requested that he be cast in the movie *My Best Girl*. They played sweethearts in the movie, and the romance went off screen.

At that time, Mary was married to Douglas Fairbanks. Her marriage to Rogers came after she divorced Fairbanks, and most of Hollywood said that the marriage would not last six months. They remained married until her death at age eighty-nine and raised two adopted children. Pickford owned radio station KFDI in Wichita for several years.

Buddy was in thirty-nine pictures. He was awarded the Jean Hirsholt Humanitarian Award from the Academy of Motion Picture Arts and Sciences in 1986. He also has a star on the Hollywood Walk of Fame.

Buddy died of natural causes in 1999 at age ninety-four. He is buried in Forest Lawn Cemetery in Palm Springs, California. Though time has passed, the fact has not changed that one of Hollywood's brightest stars was a Kansas boy.

DAVID DARY—HISTORIAN

Historian is a simplistic label to put on David Dary. He was born in Manhattan in 1934. One of his great-grandfathers settled there in 1865 and was an early merchant. His maternal grandfather, Archie W. Long, who was mayor at one time, owned Long Oil Company. David's parents were Russell and Ruth Long Dary of Manhattan. His mother earned a master's degree from K-State in 1926. David graduated from K-State in 1956. He also earned a graduate degree from the University of Kansas.

After graduating from K-State, he began a career with WIBW, a radio and television station in Topeka, later working in Texas. He joined CBS News in Washington, D.C., and covered the last months of the Eisenhower administration and then the Kennedy administration. Dary introduced President Kennedy's speech on the Cuban Missile Crisis on CBS. He also overflew and observed Soviet ships carrying nuclear missiles away from Cuba. In 1963, he went to NBC News to be the Washington news manager for local news. He was frequently heard anchoring NBC's *Monitor* weekend news programs. Later, he would move to New York. He helped to build the new NBC Topeka affiliate, Channel 27.

He then joined the faculty of the William Allen White School of Journalism at KU, where he earned his graduate degree. As a professor, he began to write articles and books on Kansas history. He was recruited to become the head of what is now the Gaylord College of Journalism and Mass Communications at the University of Oklahoma in Norman. He retired after eleven years and is now professor emeritus.

As a historian and writer, this author counts a handful of people as heroes in the research and documentation of western United States and Kansas history. David Dary is first on this author's list, which includes Stan Hoig, Dr. Jim Hoy and Dr. H. Craig Minor. The legacy that David Dary has produced is impressive.

In an interview, Dary said, "I would not consider myself a crusader or anything like that." In the same vein, this author has said many times that Texans have an appreciation of their state history. A lot of state history is required in schools in Texas, and it has been stated by Dary as being "not the case in Kansas." Dary believes that Kansas should follow the example of Texas and require state history be taught in grade, middle and high schools and right into college. A belief that I acquired years ago is that it is so important to know the roots and where we come from. Kansas history is as colorful as any, and there is so much that is yet to be uncovered.

Dary's first book, *The Buffalo Book* (1974), went in depth on the importance of the buffalo to Native Americans and the role buffalo played in the West. As of this writing, Dary has published twenty-seven books on Kansas and western history. Most commonly found is *True Tales of Old Time Kansas* and its sequel, *More Tales of Old Time Kansas*. One of his most popular works is *Cowboy Culture* (1981), which covers five hundred miles of the cowboy. The number of articles and other books are not counted, but as long as he lives and investigates stories, the material piles up for his next book.

Cowboy Culture won a Wrangler Award from the National Cowboy Hall of Fame and Western Heritage Center. It also won a Spur Award from the Western Writers of America and was nominated for a Pulitzer Prize. He has won two Spur Awards and Two Wrangler Awards, as well as the Owen Wister Lifetime Achievement Award, Arrell Gibson Award and has been inducted into the Kansas Cowboy Hall of Fame. He is a member of and former member of numerous academic and professional journalism organizations. He served on the board of directors of the Kansas State Historical Society for twenty years. Dary is past president of the Western Writers of America, a formal council member of the Western History Association, and past president and board chairman of Westerners International.

Dary has been a longtime collector of books, pamphlets and ephemera on Kansas and the West and became an appraiser of such items in the 1980s. He still adds to his library. Dary and his wife, Sue, who is an artist and former student of K-State, live in Norman, Oklahoma.

Author's note: Since this story was written, David Dary died. Thus passed one of the most respected Kansas historians.

CAPTAIN DONALD K. ROSS, BEVERLY—MEDAL OF HONOR

Donald K. Ross was born near Beverly and Healy, in Lincoln County. He spent time in the area, and his grandparents had a farm there, but his life before the navy is so overshadowed that it is hard to find him. The story always picks up when he joined the navy in 1929, when he became a machinist's mate. His first assignment was to the USS *Henderson*. His first action was in 1931 while serving on a hospital ship, the USS *Relief*, in Nicaragua. He served on the USS *Brant* (a mine sweeper), USS *Simpson* (a destroyer), the USS *Minneapolis* (a cruiser) and as a warrant officer machinist on the USS *Nevada* (a battleship).

On December 7, 1941, the Japanese attacked Pearl Harbor, Hawaii, and the *Nevada* was badly damaged. Ross battled the smoke, heat and fire in the effort to power up the ship and get underway. He ordered his men to safety and performed his duties blinded until he lost consciousness. After being rescued, he went back in, refusing medical attention until forced back out by order of his superiors. The *Nevada* was the only battleship to get into action during the attack. Ross was awarded the Medal of Honor by Admiral Nimitz on April 18, 1942.

His citation reads: "When his station in the forward dynamo room became almost untenable due to smoke, steam, and heat, he forced his men to leave that station and performed all the duties himself until blinded and unconscious. Upon being rescued and resuscitated, he returned and secured the forward dynamo room and proceeded to the aft dynamo room, where he was again rendered unconscious by exhaustion. Upon recovering consciousness, he returned to his station, where he remained until directed to abandon it."

Ross was involved in the Battle of Normandy and Operation Dragoon, reaching the rank of lieutenant by the end of World War II. He subsequently attained the ranks of lieutenant commander, commander and, because of his service time and awards, upon his retirement was raised to captain.

Donald K. Ross was the first man to receive the Congressional Medal of Honor at Pearl Harbor. He received the following awards: Medal of Honor, Purple Heart, Navy Commendation Medal, Second Nicaraguan Campaign Medal, American Defense Medal with FLEET clasp, Asiatic-Pacific Campaign Medal with Five Battle Stars, European-African-Middle Eastern Campaign Medal with Two Battle Stars, World War II Victory Medal, Navy Occupation Medal with ASIA clasp and National Defense Service Medal.

Captain Ross retired after twenty-seven years of service aboard every type of surface ship then afloat. Upon leaving the navy, he retired to a farm in Port Orchard, Washington, with his wife, Helen. He raised four children: Fred, Robert, Penny and Donna. He wrote a book about his fellow Medal of Honor recipients. *Men of Valor* was published in 1980.

Captain Ross died of a heart attack in Bremerton, Washington, on May 27, 1992, at age eighty-one. His ashes were scattered at sea. In 1997, a guided missile destroyer, the USS *Ross*, was commissioned in his honor. The USS *Ross* was one of the ships that launched cruise missiles at the airfield in Syria, from where nerve gas attacks had originated in April 2017.

Through the efforts of fellow Beverly natives Joe Cassell and Jack Meili, the Kansas legislature passed a bill that was signed by Governor Brownback on March 22, 2011, designating K-18 in Lincoln County as the Donald K. Ross Memorial Highway. A forty-mile stretch of the highway from the U.S. 81/K-18 junction through western Ottawa and Lincoln Counties to the Russell County line was named in his honor.

CLEMENTINE PADDLEFORD

Clementine Paddleford was born on September 27, 1898, near Stockdale on a 240-acre farm that is now under the waters of Tuttle Creek Reservoir. She graduated from Manhattan High School in 1916, then went on to Kansas State Agriculture College (KSU), where she graduated in 1921. She obtained a degree in industrial journalism. After working for local newspapers and being involved in many organizations in college, she moved to New York City. She felt that she was a failure there, and after attending a wedding in Chicago and staying with a friend, she went to work for the Agricultural News Service and Milk Market News.

It was not long before her writing talents and her confident personality caught the attention of other papers. Upon moving to New York City, she entered Columbia School of Journalism and took night classes at New York University. She made her expenses by reviewing books for the *Journal Publication Administration* and the *New York Sun*. She soon became a food writer for many publications, including the *New York Herald Tribune*, *New York Sun*, *New York Telegram*, *Farm & Fireside* and *This Week*.

Clementine wrote about local cuisines and was soon traveling over fifty thousand miles a year when most food editors stuck to their desks. She believed that everyone had a desire for the local dishes that they grew up with and that each region had its own specialties. She became a private pilot and owned a Piper Cub in order to get around faster. There was nowhere she would not go to find out about food and new recipes, and many faithful readers sent her their favorites. She dined in Duncan Hines's

Clementine Paddleford. *Courtesy of the Clementine Paddleford Collection, Kansas State University Library.*

kitchen, at the queen's inauguration, on the USS *Skipjack* submarine, on the KATY railroad and at a hobo convention. She poked her head into restaurants all over the nation.

Clementine's mother had impressed on her the saying, "Never grow a wishbone, daughter, where your backbone ought to be," a saying that served her well when she was diagnosed with throat cancer. The removal of her larynx and vocal cords could have been the end of a reporter's career. She agreed to a partial laryngectomy, which allowed her to still use her voice, but she breathed through a hole in her throat. She wore a black ribbon over the hole for the rest of her life.

Clementine has been lost to us because of her successors like Julia Childs and the whole new following of food writers. When she died in 1967, she left her personal papers to Kansas State University. The 363 boxes lay uninventoried for thirty years. She was a pack rat, keeping everything from matchbook covers to invitations. Finally, funding was provided for a cataloging of the contents in 2001. A small showing was done at that time, opening to scholars the world of dining fifty years previous.

Clementine had many sayings, but her favorite was "There is no perfume in the world like the springtime smell of prairie air."

Clementine's works include *Patchwork Quilts* (1928), *A Dickens Christmas Dinner* (1933), *Twelve Favorite Dishes, with Duncan Hines and Gertrude Lynn* (1947), *Recipes from Antoine's Kitchen: The Secret Recipes of the Century-Old Restaurant in the French Quarter of New Orleans* (1948), *A Flower for My Mother* (1959), *How America Eats* (1960) and *Clementine Paddleford's Cook Young Cookbook* (1966). Her posthumous works are *The Best American Cooking* (1970) and *American Food Writing: An Anthology with Classic Recipes* (1970).

Clementine Paddleford was descended from families from the Revolutionary War. She is buried in the Grandview–Mill Creek–Stockdale Cemetery in Riley, Kansas.

BIG CHIEF MANUFACTURING— CLINTON JOHN KREHBIEL

CJ, as he was called by everyone, started to build a prefabricated Quonset-style building for agriculture and many other uses in Moundridge starting in 1950. He was born in McPherson on February 13, 1920, the son of Rudolf R. and Anna Stuckey Krehbiel. He graduated from Moundridge High School in 1938 and married Arleen Lillia in August 1942. Shortly after their marriage, he joined the navy and served in the South Pacific from 1943 to 1945.

Upon returning home, the couple made their home in Moundridge. CJ and his father started Big Chief Manufacturing Company in Moundridge, creating fabricated components for the Quonset or "round top" buildings that were similar to those used in the military. It is a good assumption that CJ was influenced by these buildings during his time in the navy.

He moved the business to larger facilities in Hutchinson in 1950 and in the process created a separate retail division. The two businesses ran out of the same location but as two separate entities. The newly created Big Chief Sales was run by R.R. Krehbiel. It is assumed that dealerships were sold around the country, but the papers of the company are hard to find, and this is only an assumption.

Salesman models of the superstructure of the buildings are known to exist, with one model being sold in a toy auction in 2017. The company was located north of Highway 50 in east Hutchinson at 3501 East Fourth, across from the Hutchinson airport.

In 1959, the factory site was bought by Farmland Industries and was in business there until 1986. The plant was leased to Jackson Ice Cream and Republic Paperboard. Farmland sold the property to Go Investments LLC in 2000, and it was a storage facility from 2000 to 2006. The property was then sold to Superior Boiler Works, which manufactures industrial boilers.

CJ built the Starlight Skating Center in Salina in 1963. He and his wife, Arlene, managed the rink until their retirement in 1984, when son Roger took over. CJ died on November 28, 2007, and is buried in Mound Township Cemetery.

In travels around the country, it would not be unusual to look at a round-top building and see the Big Chief logo on the end.

COBALT BOATS

"We don't want to be the biggest boat building company, just the best"— pretty big words from a boy who grew up in Independence, Kansas. But he made good on those words, and you won't find many who disagree. Of course, you would think that just about anywhere where there is big water would be the place to establish a boat building company, taking advantage of the old salts who spent a lifetime on the water—nope. You do it with a loyal workforce that is heavy on farm and Kansas ingenuity and work ethic, and that is what Pack St. Clair does.

Pack's father was a lumber salesman, calling on lumber dealers in three states. Pack and his father spent a lot of time growing up in a Lone Star boat going to lakes all over Kansas and Oklahoma. Attending the University of Kansas, Pack was a football star, but after college, what does a young man do to stay living in an area where he loved hunting, fishing and living? He tried being a lumber salesman, like his dad, but that was just not a job that appealed to him for the long term. But he had determination, ambition and a good neighbor who became his partner. They started building big fiberglass slides, but not the playground type of slide. The new partners built the twelve-row slides forty feet high that people would ride down on gunny sacks. The business was pretty good for a while until the insurance company called the partners and told them that the slides were a bit too dangerous for people who did not ride them the way they were supposed to, and they needed to quit and build something else.

Since they were experienced in building things out of fiberglass, they turned to their love of boats and decided to build their own. At first, they copied some boats, and their first efforts were "pretty snazzy." They contacted a boat designer and had a sixteen- and eighteen-foot tri-hull design made. Initially, these models were their only original design. Purchasing tooling from a company in Dallas that had gone out of business, they got down to the business of building boats. Their boats were introduced in 1968, and Pack went on the road to sell their products. With a double-decked trailer holding two boats behind his car, he would be out for a month sometimes, attending shows and signing up dealers. He showed up to a national show in Chicago where he was able to see all the industry on display, and he did not stand out. He did not sell one boat or sign one dealer at the Chicago boat show.

After seeing the names and products, he came home and scrapped their line of boats and started over. Seeing that the mid-size and price market was full, the company needed to fill a niche—and that was at the high end. At this time, his partner had had enough of the business and sold his share to Pack. Starting over in Chanute, Pack's boats were called Kustom Craft. When he tried to register the name before the IMTEC show, his lawyer informed him that the name was taken. He already had his brochures ordered, so he called the printer to see how much time he had to come up with a new name. He had to have it by noon that day.

Thinking for ten minutes, he remembered that the name Cobalt was a catalyst used in the fiberglass process that causes resins to cure. He called and put the name Cobalt on the brochure. Then he went home, where his wife said it was "the dumbest name he could choose since it was part of a cancer treatment." Regardless, they headed to the big IMTEC show in Chicago and spent four days standing outside the boat, showing it to anyone who showed interest. They came home and started building their new boat.

Neodesha had an oil refinery close down, and the town owned a large tract of land that it was turning into an industrial park. With incentives, Cobalt Boats moved to Neodesha. With a new partner, the company built a high-end boat that was not only good looking but would perform as well. They needed to get sales moving, so Pack took one to San Francisco to the boat show outside the Cow Palace. By this time, the only California dealer was in Fullerton. Pack called on dealers around the state with little success. He learned he could not get into the Cow Palace for a display and made a deal with a Mobil station across the street, parking next to the sidewalk. He got attention.

Pack now has dealers all over the country and the world and employs around eight hundred workers. He credits the work ethic and ingenuity of the farmers and rural people who come from fifty miles around to work there. He has become a major part of the southeast Kansas economy and has developed another interest—wine. He now makes Cobalt Wine.

In 2017, Cobalt Boats was sold to Malibu Boats. Malibu Boats expected to continue production in Neodesha under the Cobalt name.

DIXON ZTR

Before the Dixon ZTR (zero turning radius) mower, there were others on the market. Of course, there is more to the story than the well-known product. It started in Wichita in the aircraft industry when W.O. Dixon had a machine shop. The aircraft industry is one that is up and down, and subcontractor work is a volatile business. In 1951, Dixon sold his company to the Oklahoma Can Company, and the company name changed to Olin-Dixon, with the new owners retaining the Dixon name.

W.O. bought a cattle ranch near Grove, Oklahoma. He had been tending his cattle for eleven years when the Olin-Dixon Company decided to close its doors. While ranching, Dixon had started a pipeline equipment and supply company in Tulsa, Oklahoma. The company approached Dixon about him buying his company back. He decided to do it, and several years later, his son K.O. Dixon joined him.

K.O. joined his father as plant manager in 1967. K.O. had a degree in production management from Oklahoma State University. W.O. had originally expanded operations to Coffeyville in 1948. In the 1970s, the aircraft industry had gone into a major reduction, and at that time, W.O. decided to retire. This left K.O. without a job or any clear idea of what he would do.

Looking around for something he could manufacture, K.O. discovered a company in Lawrence that held a patent on a zero turning radius lawn mower. Several models were manufactured by other companies, but they all used hydraulic transmissions and were expensive. The unique patent for a mechanical transmission model in Lawrence seemed inexpensive to build and a perfect catch.

K.O. did not know anything about lawn mowers, but that did not stop him, and he formed Dixon Industries and started building lawn mowers. But there was a little hurdle. The company that held the patent was on the auction block. K.O. went to the auction but did not have enough money for the assets and the rights of the company. He went home disappointed. Then the phone rang. It was the bank that owned the assets, asking K.O. if he would still be interested in buying the company. He told them that he did not have enough money. He was told to come up for a meeting, and he came back with the company.

The company went into production in 1974 and was going full speed in 1975 with twenty-five employees. Success was not overnight, but in the first year, the company produced 760 mowers. It took a while to get a distribution system put together. The company went to major industry trade shows to get its name out and recruit distributors. By the end of 1978, the company had expanded fourfold and was a leading producer of lawn equipment.

The company was going great in the 1980s, when the decision was made to join a company that had greater capital to build and market the line. The company was sold to the Coleman Company. The transaction was most notable for the fact that it did not affect the Coffeyville operations. For all the fears of turning over control of the company to a larger concern, Coleman retained K.O. as its manager of the Coffeyville operations.

The affiliation with Coleman gave the company the opportunity to double its operations, but four years after the acquisition, the Coleman Company was bought by McAndrews and Forbes in a leveraged buyout. That meant the company was once again for sale. It was a nervous time for K.O. and the company. In 1990, the company was bought by Blount International Inc. of Montgomery, Alabama. Fortunately, the same thing happened when Dixon was folded into Blount's Outdoor Products Group along with three other companies (Oregon Cutting Systems, ICS and Fredrick Mfg. Corp.). In the 1990s, Blount exited the construction business and concentrated on manufacturing enterprises. Dixon kept distributors and dealers intact and eclipsed the sales records of the first half of the decade with over $40 million in sales. The company expanded into many other countries and had a total of 161,000 square feet of manufacturing space. In late 1996, the company was acquired by Husqvarna. It announced the closing down of the Dixon division, and no more blue Dixon mowers were sold after 2004. It was a severe disappointment not only for the employees but also the distributors, dealers and customers.

FUNK BROTHERS

Joe and Howard Funk were born within thirty minutes of each other in Akron, Ohio, on September 17, 1910. The brothers showed a knack for all things mechanical and excelled in drafting and shop classes in school. They were both attracted to aviation, and the Akron area was a hotbed of aircraft activity in the early twentieth century. But their parents were not thrilled by their choice of interest and set them up in the grocery business. This, however, provided a means of financing the dreams that they had to fly.

The first aircraft they designed and finished was on July 2, 1934, and looked like a redesigned Piper Cub. The first engine that they chose was a Szekely, which was a three-cylinder radial engine and notoriously unreliable. As a replacement, they quickly modified a Ford four-cylinder engine, and it proved more reliable. The engine was mounted in an inverted position. The Ford motor with the Funk modifications was so reliable that it was installed in the next sixty airplanes they built.

In 1940, the brothers asked the Akron business community for backing to build the company and get it out of the back room of the grocery. With $78,000 in capital, they moved into a four-story abandoned schoolhouse on the northwest corner of the Akron Airport. In the later part of 1940, production slowed because it was determined that the Ford engines required an excessive amount of maintenance. At that time, they switched to a Lycoming air-cooled engine. A factory flaw was found in the Lycoming engines, and while the company shut down for the problem to be rectified, one of the creditors became nervous and forced them into bankruptcy.

Help came from Coffeyville in the form of oil field suppliers Bill and Raymond Jensen. The Funks were anxious to rebuild and get back into business and agreed to support from the Jensens. The plant was put south of Coffeyville, which was actually in Oklahoma, but the impact on employment was felt in Kansas as well. Their first order shipped was three planes that went to South America. This was just at the start of World War II with the bombing of Pearl Harbor. They picked up contracts to get them through the war. At the end of the war, they had plans to get back into full production, but there were numerous hurdles. In 1945, the cost of a new Funk was $37,000, but the government was selling surplus planes, and there was a general downturn for all aircraft companies for a few years after the war. The company only sold a few dozen planes in 1947, and in 1948, production closed down on airplanes for good.

The Funks turned their sights on tractors when they could no longer sell airplanes. Ford had produced the 8N tractor that had only thirty horsepower and pulled a two-bottom plow. Farmers wanted more power in the compact tractor and wanted to pull a three-bottom plow. The brothers developed adapter kits to replace the four-cylinder with six- and eight-cylinder Ford engines. The one-hundred-horsepower flathead V-8 engine gave the tractor new popularity.

There was a potential problem, however. Ford considered suing the boys because of the popularity of the Funk conversion. Ford threatened to stop providing the standard factory warranty on the engines purchased for use in Funk tractors. The Funk conversion was used on around eight thousand tractors, with the majority being the six-cylinder engines. Cooler heads prevailed at Ford, and the new four-cylinder engines removed from the tractors were shipped back to Ford in the same crates that the six- and eight-cylinder engines came in. This also gave Ford time to develop the higher horsepower NAA, and this spelled the end of the Funk conversion.

But this did not stop the Funk brothers from continuing in business. They went on to design and sell PTO units and transmissions. The plant did move to the airport outside Coffeyville, and today one hangar is all that is left of it. What once was the Funk Aircraft Company and then the tractor conversion company and then the transmission company still exists today. The company

8N Ford-Funk museum display. *Courtesy of Amy Roesky, Coffeyville Aviation Museum.*

8N Ford-Funk conversion. *Courtesy of Amy Roesky, Coffeyville Aviation Museum.*

Funk airplane. *Courtesy of Amy Roesky, Coffeyville Aviation Museum.*

Funk airplane on display. *Courtesy of Amy Roesky, Coffeyville Aviation Museum.*

was sold to Gardner-Denver, then to Cooper Industries and is now a part of John Deere. The plant had a contract for producing Ford industrial engines for a while.

Howard died in 1995, and Joe died in 2004. They left a legacy to the Coffeyville community. There are still many Funk airplanes flying, and many are at Oshkosh every year. There are also many collectors of the Funk-Ford conversion tractors.

HAROLD BELL WRIGHT

Pittsburg, Kansas, has claim to the residency of American author Harold Bell Wright. Wright was a writer of fiction, essays and nonfiction during the first half of the twentieth century. His work is largely forgotten other than his book *The Shepherd of the Hills*. It is believed that he was the first author to sell one million copies of a novel and the first to make one million dollars from writing fiction.

Between 1902 and 1942, Wright wrote nineteen books, several stage plays and many magazine articles. More than fifteen movies were made or claim to have been made from Wright's stories. This includes Gary Cooper's first major movie, *The Winning of Barbara Worth* (1926), and the John Wayne movie *The Shepherd of the Hills* (1941).

Born on May 5, 1872, in Rome (Oneida County), New York, he was married to Frances Long-Wright and had three children. In his autobiography, *To My Songs*, he states that his father was a Civil War veteran and an alcoholic who "dragged his wife and children from place to place, existing from hand to mouth, sinking deeper and deeper as the years passed into the slough of wretched poverty." His mother paid attention to the children and taught them moral principles and read to them from the Bible, Shakespeare, *Pilgrim's Progress* and "The Song of Hiawatha."

From his mother, he learned the beauties of nature. A neighbor taught Wright to draw and paint. When Wright was eleven, his mother died and his father abandoned the children. For the rest of his childhood, he lived with various relatives and strangers, mostly in Ohio.

Wright found odd jobs and frequently slept under bridges and in haystacks. Late in his teens, he found employment painting both art and houses. In what he called his "pre-preparation" at Hiram College in Hiram, Ohio, he became a minister for the Church of Christ (Disciples of Christ) in Pierce City, Missouri. He claimed he did not set out to become a minister, but the job and the church found him.

Harold Bell Wright, postcard. *Author's collection.*

Wright moved to Pittsburg, Kansas, in the winter of 1897–98 and pastored the Christian Church there. While there, he wrote a melodramatic story titled "That Printer of Udell's." He intended to read a chapter each week to his congregation. However, before he was able to read it to his congregation, it was published in serial form in the *Christian Century*, the official journal of that denomination. He despised the serial form that was published, but parishioners enjoyed the story. They enjoyed it so much he was encouraged to publish it in book form.

It was his second novel, *The Shepherd of the Hills*, set in the Branson, Missouri region, that established him as an author. Leaving Pittsburg in 1902, he ended up in California. In a church history, his salary was stated as $800 per year with a membership of 250 at the Pittsburg Christian Church. He lived at 412 West Kansas. Efforts were made to preserve the house as a local landmark.

Pittsburg State University has a large collection of Harold Bell Wright's published works.

LIEUTENANT JG JAMES ALLEN MAXWELL— GODDARD

Kansans have always been in the service of the country through war and peace. Jim Maxwell was an athletic, well-liked youth in the Goddard community. He graduated from Goddard High School in 1952 and received a Bachelor of Arts degree in business administration from Friends University in Wichita in 1955. He married Shirley Stewart Chestnut on July 19, 1957, at the Naval Air Station Chapel at Corpus Christi, Texas.

He joined the U.S. Navy and became a pilot. He was assigned to Whiting Airfield in Milton, Florida, then transferred to Pensacola, Florida, where he was an instructor in the Navy Air Command. In a training flight flying a T-28 training aircraft, there was a midair collision with his other flight members. Maxwell did not survive the crash. It is not known what maneuvers they were performing when the collision occurred. Jim was in a two-seat model with Marine Second Lieutenant Thomas King. Both men resided at Pensacola Air Station.

Cadet Glenn Lee Hess was flying solo in the other T-28 and was also killed in the crash. The T-28 propeller-driven aircraft was what the navy used for training before moving into jet aircraft or other types of aircraft.

The crash occurred about ninety miles east of Mobile in the vicinity of Brewton, Alabama.

Coincidentally, at the same time, another navy pilot stationed at the same base was flying a Tiger Jet practicing acrobatics. Commander Robert M. Glascow was scheduled to take command of the Blue Angels Flying Team on November 1, 1958. The Tiger Jet blew up in midair for some unknown reason. The crashing jet set fire to a house when it came down on the beach around forty miles south of Mobile.

The loss of Lieutenant Maxwell was not only a blow to the family but the community as well. It was difficult to lose a well-liked young, confident and personable man. He left a wife and two stepdaughters, as well as his mother, brother and sisters.

Lieutenant JG James Maxwell is buried in the Barrancas National Cemetery, Pensacola, Florida.

McPHERSON WETLANDS

"The Great American Desert" is what early explorers called the central part of the United States. Finding an unending expanse of grassland and no forest was, at the least, intimidating to people moving through to the western side of the continent. Little did they realize what lay out in the vast expanse of grass. There were huge wetlands that were stopovers and home to hundreds of animal species and a treasure-trove of food for the Native tribes as they traveled the area.

The most well-known wetlands are the Cheyenne Bottoms and the Quivira. Cheyenne Bottoms is a freshwater wetland controlled now by Kansas Wildlife, Parks and Tourism. Quivira is a salt marsh and is a National Wildlife Refuge under the control of the U.S. Fish and Wildlife Service. Each is a major stopover for migratory birds, from ducks and geese to whooping cranes. But there was a third major wetland on the plains—the McPherson Wetlands.

The McPherson Wetlands covered an area from just south of Conway, down past McPherson, then Inman and reached down the Little Arkansas River to near Valley Center. The estimated coverage of the McPherson Valley Wetland was around thirty thousand acres. Water levels fluctuated with the amount of rainfall, so the water-covered areas would vary from year to year.

Draining the McPherson Wetlands. *Courtesy of the Inman Historical Museum.*

In the 1800s, the area was an economic boom to the local towns of Conway and McPherson. Hunters from Chicago, Kansas City, St. Louis and all points back east would arrive by train to shoot massive numbers of birds. Local residents would guide most of these hunters, and it was a sizeable business for the area. The locals would also market hunt. Barrel loads and wagon loads of birds were shot and put on the trains that took them back east for the meat markets.

One man described a hunt that was so successful that he was sent back to town to get a double-sided wagon to haul back all the birds. He estimated that it took around two thousand birds to fill the wagon, and when it came to town, everyone was able to take birds home for their own use from the wagon. Another guide said that he would allow hunting until noon and then stop. That gave everyone enough time to pick up all the birds they shot to take back to town. It was said that even with the huge numbers of birds shot each year, there were ample birds to return and nest.

A major portion of the wetlands were in McPherson County. The migration of Mennonite settlers and farmers into the region would soon start changing the function and look of the land. Large numbers of Mennonite settlers were being transported by the Santa Fe Railroad, and many settled in Marion, McPherson, Harvey and Reno Counties. The settlers were very astute farmers and had been allowed to follow their faith and conscience in the Ukraine by Catherine the Great. The area of the Ukraine is similar in temperament and geology to Kansas. As the change in rulers took place, the nonviolent beliefs of the Mennonite people were coming into conflict with expected military service. It soon became apparent that migrating was their only hope to stay true to their beliefs.

The Mennonites were a very thrifty and innovative agricultural people. As the land was being settled, there were early attempts to try to farm the wetland areas. Draining became a subject of conversation. Some of the areas were as small as one acre, with many as large as five and ten acres. The largest was the Big Basin, which covered several thousand acres, and that became the subject for draining and farming.

The creation of the wetlands area was originally the course of the Smoky Hill River. The river used to drain south and join the Arkansas River. Over time, the river changed course and flowed east, eventually joining the Missouri River. The resulting lowlands were a chain of shallow areas with two large lakes that averaged around five feet deep. Lake Inman is thought to be the only naturally occurring lake and the largest natural lake in Kansas. Starting around the turn of the twentieth century, the size of the wetlands has dropped 90 percent from its original size.

ERNEST DITTEMORE—DONIPHAN COUNTY

In what he describes as his favorite story, Larry Hatteberg—who filmed a regular feature called *Hatteberg's People*—fondly recalls the man who lived life as he wanted. Ernest Dittemore slept in a hole in the ground, four by ten feet to be exact. He moved in after his farmhouse burned down. Even though neighbors had bought him a mobile home, he thought that the underground home was cheaper to heat.

Ernie lived on the family homestead that his parents had acquired in 1901. His unique lifestyle and peculiar way of living made him the subject of stories all over the country. The *Chicago Tribune* described him as "a Republican, property owner, farmer, [who] owns a private airplane and an airstrip, eighty acres of land, thirty-five head of cattle, six hogs, fifteen outbuildings, and a mobile home."

Telephone messages for him were left at the city shops in Highland, where his friend Jim Gilmore would answer questions. Gilmore grew up and farmed next to Ernie and was a good friend. Gilmore would tell you that many people thought Ernie was a kook or even a mountain man, but everyone who knew Ernie liked him. Ernie was pleasant and liked to read. He was good company and liked to have good company around.

Ernie kept a 1930 Chevrolet, a 1928 McCormick-Deering tractor and a Piper Cub in different sheds. He kept his airfield mowed, and people would come out and fly their planes and model planes at his airstrip.

From the highest point on his property, you could see the Missouri River twenty miles east near St. Joseph, Missouri. His hole in the ground was five feet deep and had a plywood hatch over the entrance. There was a concrete slab over the hole. He said he could reach out the door and bring in firewood if the snow was too deep and be comfortable.

Ernie's property was near Troy, Kansas. He was a lifelong bachelor, described as toothless and sooty. He had no qualms about admitting that he did not attempt to stay clean or bathe. He was born on May 31, 1915, and died on November 14, 1995, at age eighty.

Ernie is still a topic of conversation. There is a Facebook page devoted to him, and if you ask about him at the County Historical Museum you will get a smile and a lot of Ernie Dittemore stories.

ALMON STROWGER— AUTOMATIC TELEPHONE EXCHANGE

Once Kansans saw the usage of telephones, they wanted the ability to have one. The very first phone use in Kansas was by the Leavenworth prison. The business adjacent would pick up the phone and order some cheap labor from the prison when it needed it.

A fence line phone system was installed between twelve families in Wallace County. The problem was, the phone was out of service any time someone left the gate open.

Soon there were telephone exchanges that used men as operators because the men's deeper and louder voices could be heard better than women over the static and poor-quality sound. The first switchboard was set up in Topeka in 1879. Within ninety days, fifty-two people had signed up. Soon, quality improved, and many operators were women.

This posed a problem. Almon Strowger was in the undertaking business. There is conflicting information on where this was. He had lived in El

Dorado, Topeka and Kansas City. He was all of a sudden not getting calls to do funerals. When a friend died and a new competing undertaker did the funeral, he found out that the new undertaker had an operator for a girlfriend. This set Almon about inventing the automatic telephone exchange.

Almon enlisted the services of nephew Walter Strowger near El Dorado, and the machine he designed was built by a jeweler and his assistant in Wichita. Using Walter's drawings, the device was built and the patent was applied for. There were many difficulties along the way, and Almon sold everything to finance the invention. He ended up in Chicago and found a Joseph Harris—who was also disenchanted with the phone system— to finance the invention and a new company, the Strowger Automatic Telephone Exchange Company.

Securing the patent, the new company set up an exchange in La Porte, Indiana. Ninety-nine phones at one time were on the new exchange. This was the first time a number could be called direct without the help of an operator to put the call through. The device was exhibited at the 1893 Chicago World's Fair, but the design was not yet perfected. There was room for improvement.

The first dial system based on Almon's patent was installed in city hall in Milwaukee, Wisconsin. The first system was a series of push buttons— the dial came later. The Bell Telephone Company was working on similar equipment, and some inventors from Lindsborg worked on improvement of the automatic dialing system, helping to create the dial telephone. One of the first major sales for the Strowger Automatic Telephone Exchange Company was in Germany.

Eventually, Almon sold his interests in the Strowger Automatic Telephone Exchange Company. He moved to St. Petersburg, Florida, where he went back into the undertaking business. He died in 1902.

DANE HANSEN

The name is well known in the Phillips County area, and the story is quite different from most successful businesspeople. The old adage "early to bed and early to rise makes a man healthy, wealthy and wise" was not Dane Hansen's style. Working smart was his forte. Dane was born in 1883, the son of a Danish immigrant who came to Kansas and married a young schoolteacher in Logan.

When he was young, his father owned a gristmill, and Dane would go down to the river crossing and watch for farmers bringing in wagonloads of wheat to be processed. Dane would ask them for a ride and direct them to his father's mill. Thus, he brought many prospective customers to the family mill. He went on to business school in Missouri and returned home to the family general merchandise store in 1905.

Dane and his father owned a lumberyard, and then they went into ranching and breeding Hereford cattle. When the army needed mules for World War I, Dane went around the country and bought mules. This was a great

Dane Hansen. *Courtesy of the Dane Hansen Foundation.*

business until the Armistice, when he was stuck with one hundred mules and no place to sell them. This was a dilemma he turned into an asset. He created a road construction company that utilized the mules, and the company began to grow. He built roadbeds and successfully ventured into other earth moving/gravel work. He also tried another business—oil. He started buying leases in northwest Kansas. In 1940, oil was discovered near Logan. He created his own exploration company and became the largest independent oil producer in the state.

He was civic minded and became Logan city clerk at age twenty-seven. He served the community in many different capacities. He was active in Republican politics and never missed a Republican Convention from 1920 to 1960. He did not seek the spotlight but was always an interested member.

He became a multimillionaire and could have moved his headquarters anywhere in the country. Instead, he chose to keep his office and operations centered in Logan. Although he never married, he had an interest in youth and established the Dane G. Hansen Boy Scout Camp at Kirwin. Dane was a friend of President Eisenhower and served on the board of trustees of the Eisenhower Foundation. He was a vice president of the Kansas Independent Oil and Gas Association. He was president and director of the First National Bank of Logan. He was a member of the Methodist Church and a Mason of the Thirty-Third degree of the Consistory.

Dane's business style was to sleep until 10:00 or 11:00 a.m., go to work at noon and work until 2:00 or 3:00 a.m. These hours worked well for him. With his wealth, he supported many worthwhile endeavors, including

Hansen Museum and Offices. *Courtesy of the Dane Hansen Foundation.*

scholarships and grants to organizations and students in northwest Kansas. He was elected to the Business Hall of Fame in 1990.

The Dane G. Hansen Foundation that he created has its headquarters on Main Street in Logan, and the Dane G. Hansen Memorial Plaza was conceived by the foundation. The memorial encompasses a whole block and includes a museum, community room and offices for the foundation. The square had previously been abandoned business buildings.

In 1964, his health was starting to fail, and there was a question of how his estate would be handled. He formed the foundation for his estate to be put to the best use. He died in 1965 on his eighty-second birthday. The Dane G. Hansen Museum has been called the Smithsonian of the Plains. The memorial block is a great tribute to a man who loved western Kansas, and his foundation continues his vision of helping western Kansas prosper.

EDWARD L. WIRT

In his obituary, Ed Wirt is called one of the pioneers of western Kansas. He was an early cowboy coming to the area, and from age fifteen, he worked for the Holly and Sullivan Ranch. He was a fearless, noted rider and great roper. One article says that Ed came in 1871 among the buffalo and Indians. He was born in Independence, Missouri. Living in Holly, Colorado, he married the daughter of William "Billy" Fulton and soon moved to Garden City. For a short time, he ran a general store, but he was more suited to the cattle business, which he was in for most of his life.

As Garden City and the region grew, he was soon engaged in many enterprises. He was the first to conceive of growing sugar beets in western Kansas. He bought into the Great Eastern Irrigation ditch and developed the Deerfield town site. He joined with others to form the Arkansas Valley Beet Sugar Land and Irrigation Company.

He bought into the first big body of land, amounting to over 11,400 acres. This and the Deerfield town site was sold to the U.S. Sugar and Land Company. Following this, he bought the Garden City telephone exchange and developed the enterprise alone. He soon had lines connecting to Deerfield and Lakin and heartland telephone lines connecting Ulysses, Syracuse, Scott City, Pierceville, Charleston, Eminence, Essex, Dr. Crow's, Dighton and Cimarron, later connecting to long-distance lines.

In a town listing, Edward is noted as a deputy U.S. marshal and the manager of the Red Lion livery stable. The residence in Garden City where Edward lived is still standing and is occupied. Ed was prominent in the Mason fraternal organization and was a member of all three orders. He was also chapter commander of the Blue Lodge.

Ed stayed in the cattle business his whole life until his health started to fail. He is listed in the *Herford Journal* as owner of the sire Wild Bill. He is also listed in the *American Kennel Club Book* as owner of Kansas Belle, a black and tan English setter.

Despite being a real pioneer in early western Kansas, Ed gets overshadowed and overlooked because of one daughter. Sydia Wirt was a precocious child who was the apple of her daddy's eye. She was full of energy and mischief as she grew up. One instance of her shenanigans is written when she persuaded her friend, whose father owned a hotel, to slide the full length of the banister with her to the main floor on the main staircase. The friend's father was aghast and disciplined his daughter, but Ed had a big laugh and wrote it off as childish hijinks. Her life seemed to be filled with hijinks for many years after.

Sydia, whose name was spelled many different ways over time, was known most often as "Sidi." Sidi Wirt would go on to marry four times, once becoming a Turkish

E.L. Wirt. *Courtesy of the Finney County Historical Society.*

princess. The name most often associated with her was from her second marriage to John Spreckles III of San Francisco, California. John was the son of a multimillionaire sugar importer. Sidi's one daughter, Geraldine, was with John Spreckles III, and she would go on to live a colorful life as her mother did. Geraldine even co-starred in the movie *Jezebel*, the movie for which Betty Grabel won the Oscar for Best Actress. Geraldine used the stage name Anna Jones for her role in this movie, so she does not show up as Geraldine Spreckles in the credits.

Sidi's exploits over the years gave the society pages a running serial to which papers devoted full-page displays with illustrations. Sidi is a subject for her own story.

Toward the end of Ed's life, he lived for a short time with a daughter in Hutchinson. He died of a heart attack while on a trip to Washington State.

MICHAEL C. HORNUNG—CRUST BUSTER

To quote the philosophy of K.O. Huff: "When there is a need, you just build it." Kansans have been seeing needs and building things since the state began. Michael Hornung exemplifies that creed. Born on the farm that was homesteaded by his grandfather in the 1870s near Spearville in western Kansas, Michael learned early what farming was all about. Plowing with a one-bottom plow, his dad followed with a two-bottom, and that was big farming at the time. Five acres a day was really making progress.

While Michael was serving on the local school board in the 1950s, the district was building a new gymnasium. The school was not happy with the manual fold-up basketball goals that were available at that time. Along with another farmer, Victor Classen, the two decided that there was a better way and designed and built electrically retractable goals. Both went back to the farm, but other schools heard about the goals and started contacting them to build more of these basketball goals. The pair started the E-Z Goal Company, which led both of them to leave their farming operations and build basketball goals. They eventually employed thirty people. Later, Michael sold his interest to his partner and other investors. Eventually, the company was sold to Universal Bleacher in Illinois.

With the manufacturing skills he had developed, his attention turned back to the farm. More and more farmers were leaving, and farm sizes kept growing. With the practices of western Kansas farming—which consisted of farming half the ground and leaving the other half to lay fallow for a year—there was a need to control weeds. At the time, the drag spring tooth was the standard for ground and seedbed preparation. The drag spring tooth was limited in size and difficult to move from field to field, especially when the fields were farther apart. So Michael designed a folding spring tooth. The implement was a big hit, and soon the new company was building the folding spring tooths and then folding grain drills.

The new company was named American Products, but soon the identity of the popular Crust Buster made a change of company name possible. Times allowed the company to expand its product line and expand the factory. Three factories in Spearville were eventually united into one sixty-thousand-square-foot facility, and a plant in Dodge City had ninety thousand square feet.

Changes in both the farm economy and the country's economy created huge challenges that the company has had to navigate to survive. In the 1970s, the fence-row-to-fence-row farming system and getting bigger at all costs was supported by five-dollar wheat. The energy crisis of the 1980s and the resulting raising of interest rates through the roof by the Federal Reserve created the worst farm depression since the 1930s. Many solid companies failed, and many farmers were driven into bankruptcy. In order to survive, the CrustBuster Company started to buy smaller manufacturers to diversify.

CrustBuster folding spring tooth. *Courtesy of John Blocker Farms.*

The company was renamed CrustBuster–Speed King. Acquisition of the Speed King Company expanded products into material handling, and the acquisition of Boll Buggy added the cotton handling business.

The company today does not build tillage tools. It has moved into large no-till drills (up to sixty feet), building on the market at the time of this story. The company is in many forms of seed and material handling and still is a major employer in the western Kansas region.

Michael died on June 8, 1988. His sons continued the company, and there is a permanent scholarship in Michael's name with the Southwest Community Foundation. The company is still family held, and though they have had the opportunity to sell many times, they have made a commitment to the employees and the southwest Kansas economy.

MORGANVILLE AND FEVES, FRANCE: SISTER CITIES

Morganville, founded in 1870 and named for founder Ebenezer Morgan, is located north of Clay Center and south of Clifton. Located on the Chicago Rock Island and Pacific Railroad, the original name of the post office was Della. The town prospered, as many farm towns did, and suffered the economic times of the Depression. After World War II, the population of the town was 197.

The size of the town did not change the size of the hearts of the residents. There was an organization to help war-torn Europe called Operation Democracy Program, in an effort to have cities in the United States adopt a city in Europe to help rebuild. The town soon found out about Feves, France. Feves was a small town of similar size, an agricultural town that raised grapes and produced wine.

During the war, Feves was evacuated three times, the cattle were driven away and 75 percent of the town was destroyed. There was little food, and milk for the children was scarce. Ordinarily, it was towns of larger size and resources that participated in the program. Morganville was the smallest. At a town hall meeting, two women decided that the town needed to do something to help rebuild Feves.

The movement started at that town hall meeting by "the two Velmas"— Velma Carson and Velma Young—decided that a "blow out" needed to be done to raise money to aid the town and people. The idea became the One

World Peace Festival. The festival started with a dinner at the church and then a pageant, followed by a dance. The pageant was based on the meter of "The Song of Hiawatha" and had a cast of 150. On August 27, 1948, 3,000 people attended, raising $1,000. Many more community fundraising efforts contributed to the fund.

On October 23, 1948, the first shipment of supplies left New York on the SS *Gadron Maersk*. The shipment included vegetable seeds, school supplies, sugar, canned meat and cheese. Many more shipments followed, and the people of Feves sent thank-you letters and a painted hand carving by artist Martin Thian showing a man reading the Bible and a woman napping by a fireplace. The piece is displayed in the café in Morganville today.

Time allows ties to wane, but in 2014, the two cities renewed their contact. Today, the population of Morganville is 402. The Operation Democracy Program became the International Sister Cities Program, and Morganville has the distinction of being the smallest town to participate in the program.

PEGGY HULL

Peggy Hull was the first accredited war correspondent who was a woman, and she led quite a life. But Peggy was her pen name. Born on a farm near Bennington, Kansas, on September 30, 1890, her name was Eleanor Henrietta Goodnough. She grew up in Marysville and later moved to Junction City. She was a fan of investigative reporter Nellie Bly. Peggy honed her writing skills in high school. She applied for a job at the *Junction City Sentinel* and was told that the reporter job had been filled but that if she was not afraid about her fingernails, she could go to work as a typesetter. She got the job, and her first break came when a fire occurred in town and there was no one to cover the event.

Reporting on the fire proved her talent, and she was reassigned as a reporter. Between 1909 and 1916, she worked for papers in Colorado, California, Hawaii and Minnesota. She was reporting for the *Cleveland Plain Dealer* in 1916 and was assigned to cover the Ohio National Guard in Mexico. The soldiers were patrolling the border under General John J. Pershing in the hunt for Pancho Villa. Villa had made a notorious raid on the U.S. side of the border in New Mexico. Once there, Peggy started writing for the *El Paso Morning Times*, where her reporting on Pershing's return is considered one of the most accurate accounts of the event.

Peggy Hull in uniform for reporting on World War I. *Courtesy of the Spencer Research Library, University of Kansas.*

In 1917, she convinced the *Morning Times* editor to assign her to France to cover World War I. At the time, the War Department did not allow women journalists to be war correspondents, but through her acquaintance with General Pershing, she was able to spend a month at an artillery training camp. Envious male reporters in France saw to it that she was recalled to Paris, and she returned to the United States not very happy.

In the summer of 1918, she traveled to Washington, D.C., where she received accreditation with the help of General Peyton C. March from El Paso. There was always resistance to females going to the front, and generally it required an officer to accompany them to make sure they did not get too close to the fighting.

In World War II, she complained that her assignments were always too far away from the heavy fighting. She was sent to cover Siberia, Shanghai and several Pacific islands. Even though she was frustrated with the effort to keep her away from the heavy fighting, the readers loved her view on the events. A soldier writing in 1944 said, "You will never realize what those yarns of yours...did to this gang....You made them know that they were not forgotten."

In 1953, Peggy retired to Carmel Valley, California. Her career allowed her to travel all over the world. She once stated, "I never tire of doing this work." Peggy put a feminine focus and human aspect on her stories and was widely respected for her work. She wrote of the daily life of the soldiers, the day-to-day things that the folks back home appreciated knowing. She died in California of breast cancer in 1967.

Peggy was another of those Kansas people who had a dream or ambition and went out and made their mark. She not only blazed a trail for women but also left a legacy for Kansans to be proud of. The University of Kansas has Peggy's papers. A biography of her life was written by Wilda M. Smith and Eleanor A. Bogart. *The Wars of Peggy Hull* is published by Texas Western Press.

PRESIDENT THEODORE ROOSEVELT

Teddy Roosevelt may have been from New York, but he did ranch in North Dakota and was a rugged outdoorsman. During his presidential campaigns, in office and out of office, he was fond of Kansas. During his lifetime, he visited Kansas many times and had a warm friendship with Emporia newspaperman William Allen White. In the archives at the Theodore Roosevelt Center at Dickinson State University, there are many letters and telegrams that went between the two men. Teddy was a frequent visitor at White's home, Red Rocks. White was instrumental in helping Teddy form the Bull Moose Party, and they were fast friends until Teddy's death at age sixty-one.

In the spring of 1903, Teddy went on a four-thousand-mile whistle stop tour in the American West. The tour lasted eight weeks. During his western trek, he visited Yellowstone, the Grand Canyon and Yosemite. It was a grand break from the stress of politics in Washington. During the trip, he stopped at many Kansas towns and gave a short speech at each one. On Sunday, May 3, he was scheduled to be in Sharon Springs. He expressed the desire to go to church in a church building and take time to meet people and relax.

With the knowledge that Teddy wanted to spend a day in Sharon Springs, the welcoming committee got started sprucing up the town and making plans for the influx of visitors that the presence of the president would bring. Big plans were made for a huge church service in a tent that was rented from Kansas City. Upon hearing of the preparations, Teddy reiterated that he wanted a simple church service within the walls of a church. So the tent went back, and the new Methodist church was chosen as the best and largest that the town could provide.

When Teddy's train arrived, it was an impressive sight. There were six gleaming private cars—first a baggage car, then the Atlantic (a car filled with wood and leather with a complete barbershop), then the Gilsey (a dining car stocked with cigars and champagne), then the Senegal (a Pullman car carrying reporters, photographers, telegraphers, and Secret Service), followed by the Texas (carrying White House staff and guests) and the president's own Elysian, which was a gleaming Gilded Age Pullman car sporting seventy feet of solid mahogany, velvet deep cushion seats, sinking deep furniture, a kitchen staffed by the Pennsylvania Railroad star chef, a dining room, a stateroom with giant picture windows, and a large rear platform.

He rode horseback over the prairie and took a stroll on the plains that those who accompanied him swore was twenty miles and he claimed five. The town of 170 swelled to over 2,000 overnight. Cafés were opened temporarily in every store to handle the crowd. The local paper chastised and "roundly condemned" those "opportunists" who took the standard twenty-five-cent meal and doubled it to fifty cents.

Taking his place in the church, Teddy made room for a couple of young ladies who could not find seats, and one asked him "if I knew which one was the President?" He sang loudly and enjoyed the service that was conducted by every pastor in town except the one whose church it was. He roundly greeted old soldiers and others, and the phrases "bully" and "dee-lighted, sir," were heard throughout his visits with the crowd. The Secret Service agents who were with him all along the way were busy looking out for him because he wanted to shake hands with everyone who showed up to see him.

President Theodore Roosevelt at Osawatomie. *Courtesy of the Kansas State Historical Society.*

He exclaimed "there are 170 people in this town and I have shook hands with 700 and won't quit until I am finished." At the event, there was a girl named Pearl Gorsch, who asked him if he would like a baby badger that she and her brother had captured. He said he would, and soon a two-week-old badger was delivered to him. Teddy posed for a picture with the new pet and was delighted that it would nibble at his fingers and hiss like a teapot. The Kansas badger joined the menagerie of pets at the White House. When the badger grew too big and surly, it was given to the Bronx Zoo.

On his departure the next day, Roosevelt expressed his gratitude for his refreshing visit. "You can tell the people of Russell Springs that I enjoyed my visit immensely. The church was impressive, the sermon was fine, and the singing of the choir good. ... I had a corking good horseback ride, I had a corking good time!" During this trip, Teddy visited Dorrance, St. Marys, Sharon Springs, Victoria, WaKeeny, Kansas City, Abilene, Ellis, Salina, Wamego, Chapman, Ellsworth, Russell, Hays, Oakley, Topeka, Junction City and, of course, Emporia, where he visited and stayed with William Allen White.

RORY LEE FEEK

Rory Lee Feek was born in Atchison in 1966. His father, Robert, worked for a railroad service company. Rory's favorite time growing up was the time spent in Highland. The family moved around a lot, and it was hard for Rory to really feel like he was a part of a community. But Highland was his favorite.

Rory was inspired by Robert, whose playing and singing let him work in a lot of local country bands. Rory has many memories of riding in his father's old Buick. To Rory, Robert was a great singer, and this added to inspiration from Merle Haggard, Don Williams and other traditional country artists.

Rory put in two tours with the marines, and when he got out, he moved to Dallas, Texas. There he played in nightclubs and then moved to Nashville.

Rory was a talented songwriter as well as a singer. His first single released was Colin Raye's "Someone You Used to Know." It became a number-five hit on the charts in 1999. Clay Walker had a top-five hit with Rory's "The Chain of Love." Rory went on writing for many artists in the 2000s—Mark Wills, Kenny Chesney, Terri Clark, Randy Travis, Lori Morgan and Tracy Bird, the latter of whom came out with the single "The Truth About Men." The first number-one hit was Blake Shelton's "Some Beach," which was co-written with Paul Overstreet.

Rory was seen by an Indiana woman at a writers' showcase at a local Nashville restaurant. Joey Martin grew up in Indiana in a family that was very musical. She was smitten and says she knew that someday they would be a couple. It was not until two years later that they met, and it was instantaneous for Rory as well. They married on June 5, 2002.

Near the farm where they lived in 2007, Joey opened a restaurant with Rory's sister. Rory's friend came into the restaurant one day and heard the two of them singing. He was immediately impressed and suggested that they enter the CMA TV talent show *Can You Duet*. They won third place but made their mark as a duo on the country scene. Rory then founded Giantslayer Records, and their first album came out in 2008.

After that, Joey + Rory started to tour the country and became guests on the Grand Ole Opry. They had a radio program on WSM 650 AM in Nashville. Then they started the *Joey + Rory Show* on RFD TV. The TV program showcased their life living the dream and sharing their talents, as well as the talents of their friends and neighbors. Rory also developed and shot a movie about the Civil War and a real-life story that happened at that time. The movie's name was *Josephine*.

Rory's two daughters from a previous marriage adopted Joey as their own mother. Joey and Rory had their only daughter together, Indiana, who has Down syndrome, soon after Joey received a diagnosis of cervical cancer.

Including their friends and fans, Rory kept a regular blog, *This Life I Live*. This journal kept everyone informed of all the ups and downs of the cancer treatment. When the cancer treatments did not work anymore, it became a letter of love to all the fans as to how Joey embraced the love and faith that she had. The last goals that Joey had were to see her father become a believer in Jesus Christ, make it to Christmas 2015 for Indiana and make it to Indiana's second birthday. She made all three goals.

To those who loved the Feeks, it was a painful and prayerful journey, still hoping against hope for a miracle cure. In the end, Joey wished to travel home to be with her eternal father, and she made that goal on March 4, 2016.

During the last months of Joey's life, the duo was nominated for a Grammy Award for their song "If I Needed You" in the Best Country Duo/Group category. They did not win, losing to Little Big Town, but they said the honor of the nomination was enough. There was a lot of press and grief in the country music community, and the fans were powerful through the long story; it is often overlooked that this started in Kansas.

Rory Feek and his wife, Joey, in a porch swing at their home. *Courtesy of Rory Feek.*

Marcy Jo's Café. Rory's sister Marcy and Joey at a segment for the *Joey + Rory Show*; note the Hiland, Kansas sign. *Courtesy of Rory Feek.*

But Rory's story has not ended. Life goes on, and the chronicle of the life of Rory and little Indiana continues. In the studio barn that Joey + Rory built on the farm, a cowboy church started to use the facility. It was also host for specials that looked back at the history of the *Joey + Rory Show* with the friends and people who worked to put on the show every week on RFD TV.

As time goes on, Indiana has grown, and a one-room schoolhouse has been added to the property so she can go to school close to home and with area friends. Rory has continued exploring his talent and works on new ideas. In a visit with owner of RFD TV Patrick Goetsch, Rory was telling him about ideas for new television shows, and Patrick offered Rory a new job as creative director for evening programming with the network.

Fans will be looking forward to all of the new creations that Rory and Indiana will be doing in the future. Makes a Kansan proud.

RANDY SCHLITTER—RANS DESIGNS

Wichita is the Air Capital of the World, but there is another company that builds airplanes and is very successful: RANS Aircraft in Hays. It's not the place you would think of when looking for an airplane. The RANS aircraft was the brainchild of native Randy Schlitter, and the inspiration of the company and the airplane goes back to what the Wright brothers were doing: building bicycles.

It starts like many tales of a kid dreaming of flying as he is pushed by the wind, and in Hays, there is a lot of wind. Randy had an idea of building a sail plane. Think of it as Wind Wagon Smith meets the twentieth century. He designed a three-wheel sail trike in both double- and single-seated models.

It was said that the sail trikes could get up to highway speeds and have been known to pass cars on the road.

The RANS Company was set up to build sail trikes and did for several years. Building a better bicycle soon caught Randy's interest, and he designed a recumbent-style bicycle. The company grew and more models were designed, and the company soon had a faithful following from the bicycling fraternity. Some of the models that RANS produced were the rocket, Stratus, Streamer and Velocity. The bikes found a home in the baby boomers group because of the comfort factor. The biggest age group buying recumbent bicycles are the over forty crowd.

By 1997, the RANS had sold about six hundred recumbents across the country and overseas. The bikes are high quality and high performance. In 1983, a friend talked Randy into literally looking to the sky. He wanted him to build an ultralight airplane. This takes the Wilbur and Orville thing into real life.

Randy received training in aircraft mechanics and started to build kits for which the purchasers would finish the assembly. The planes were apparently a success. There is a thriving aircraft industry in Hays, and his planes fly all over the country. Computers help with the design work now, and partially finished components are boxed and shipped out. Shipments include the engine, tires, metal frame and fabric, all ready for the customer to assemble. These are not toys but serious airplanes.

About 70 percent of the company's business is shipped overseas. RANS has sold more than three thousand kits to forty-five countries around the world. The kit is a less expensive way for many people around the world to be able to fly. The company employs sixty people with no plans to leave Hays. It has done a couple of projects with NASA, one of which was a remotely piloted vehicle.

RANS vice president Paula Schlitter (Randy's wife) says that "the most interesting and most fun part of the business is dealing with people from all over the world." In the 1980s, the company faced a decision regarding its growth, and the choice was to stay in Hays or move to the big city. They chose Hays because it is where they want to raise their kids and the people are so great.

But what about the bicycle business? That is another chapter in the history of RANS. The bicycle division has been sold, and bicycles are built in Montezuma.

RANS Aircraft models built so far include Coyote, Coyote II, Courier, Sakota, Airaile, Stinger, Venttera, Raven and Outbound.

Randy Schlitter. *Courtesy of RANS Aircraft.*

RANS Airplane. *Courtesy of RANS Aircraft.*

WES JACKSON—THE LAND INSTITUTE

Wes Jackson was born on a farm near Topeka. Growing up as a farm boy, there is a lot more time to think and observe, and Wes did a lot of that. He went to Kansas Wesleyan University and earned his bachelor's degree in biology. He went on to the University of Kansas, where he earned his master's in botany, and then went to North Carolina State University, where he received his doctorate in genetics.

Wes joined the faculty of Kansas Wesleyan University in Salina. His thoughts kept turning toward the environment and agricultural issues. Soon, he accepted a position at Sacramento State University and created and served as chairman of one of the first environmental studies programs in the country.

He decided to leave academia and start The Land Institute on two hundred acres of his family homestead near Salina. Wes co-founded the institute with Dana Jackson. His main goal was to research a way to return to a natural system of agriculture as opposed to the conventional practices of the day. Topsoil was his major concern. For thousands of years, the Great Plains existed in a perennial plant system, and only when settled was the ground broken out to bring traditional farming practices from Europe and the eastern part of the country.

When J.R. Mead came to the plains, first to the Smoky Hill River and then to the Arkansas River Valley, he commented that "all the rivers were running clear and cold and without sediment. It only took 15 years of the plow for the rivers to run murky and pour out of their banks, hastening erosion."

When the Dust Bowl and drought occurred in the 1930s, topsoil loosened and, without plant and root protection, was scoured down to the hard pan. Where there had been feet of topsoil, in a few years there were only inches. Wes looked at the diversity of plants that grew together in the sod for thousands of years and started to experiment with practices and going back to what worked before the plow.

The Land Institute was formed in 1976 as a 501(c)(3) nonprofit institution. Research began on a form of agriculture known as polyculture. This simply means more than one plant variety in the field. This practice helps reduce erosion and promotes friendly soil microbe relationships. Then they attempted to breed plants that would not require replanting every year after harvesting. They worked with grains such as wheat, which was originally a grass plant.

The institute now encompasses six hundred acres, and major work is being done on creating a perennial variety of wheat. This would be wheat

Wes Jackson, founder of The Land Institute. *Courtesy of the Kansas State Historical Society.*

that is planted once and harvested for years without tillage. The overall focus is devoted to sustainable alternatives in agriculture, energy, shelter and waste management. Wes worries about the loss of topsoil and the loss of nutrients.

For many years, The Land Institute hosted an annual Prairie Festival. At the festival in 2015, Wes announced his retirement and turned over the reins of the project to the younger Fred Lutzi. Wes is now president emeritus of The Land Institute.

The institute continues to study natural ecological systems that are self-sustaining. For at least ten thousand years, humans have disrupted the natural system in order to feed the population and avoid famine. The modern system of agriculture is believed to be in danger of collapse at some point. The institute continues to investigate and develop newer ways to feed a hungry world and preserve the land.

The Land Institute near Salina is still in operation and welcomes visitors and interested parties to look at its work. Wes is still a source of inspiration and instruction. He has written many books and articles, and the Kansas State Historical Society has a collection of his papers and writings.

Wes is a PEW Conservation Scholar, a MacArthur Fellow and has received the Right Livelihood Award. In 2000, the Smithsonian included Wes as one of the "35 Who Made a Difference."

WILLIAM G. SCHAFER—
SCHAFER PLOW COMPANY

Bill Schafer started building a one-way disc plow in a little blacksmith shop at West Fifth and Washington Streets in Pratt. In a space just twenty feet by thirty feet would be the beginnings of a company that would be a big part of Pratt history and the history of agriculture. Schafer products can still be found on working farms and lined up in tree rows all over the nation. The Schafer quality and performance pushed sales, and an innovative mind pushed the company.

Bill would announce to his employees that the company was going to start building something out of the clear blue, and it would get done. Just like when, having been in the farm equipment business for years, he announced that they would start building a camper. Or when he decided that the company would produce its own high-horsepower four-wheel-drive tractor. And everything was built with an eye for quality.

Just as with the climate of agriculture, the company went through hard times and times of prosperity. It was a big employer for many years in the Pratt community. One of the lesser-known items manufactured by Schafer was a cotton stripper. At the time, cotton was not a crop that was grown in Kansas. The market that the company was supplying was the New Mexico and Texas markets, where a lot of cotton was grown. The *New Mexico Stockman* magazine stated that the Schafer product "does a more thorough job with an extremely low investment and maintenance cost." The magazine went on to say that the stripper "is equal or surpasses higher priced strippers in efficiency and performance. It makes possible clean, simplified stripping for large or small acreages."

The Schafer tractor was a nine-ton, four-wheel-drive unit that had 130 drawbar horsepower. It could pull two sixteen-foot discs or handle one hundred feet of grain drills. It could pull three eighteen-foot one-way plows. The tractor could cover 150 acres a day, which for the time was phenomenal. Bill walked in one day and told Thad Hildreth—a designer who started working after World War II painting around the shop—that they were going to build a tractor. Bill brought in a Case engine, some axles and transmissions. The design progressed from there. Tractor number one is the only model that had a Case engine; the remainder built in Pratt had International engines. Only when the assets were sold to Western Tractor Company in Kansas City did Allis Chalmers engines begin to be used.

A restored Schafer tractor. *Courtesy of Cody Garett/the* Pratt Tribune.

The day that the first Schafer tractor was unveiled—Tuesday, April 24, 1962—was a big event, and the *Hutchinson News* covered it with a story and pictures. Bill was pictured standing next to the model 18000. That tractor sold for $17,000. Representatives from Case were on hand for an explanation and to see the unit with a Case engine installed. Only three units were built with cabs, and the rest were open station models.

As result of the prospects for the new Schafer tractor, a new facility was added. In total, the company only built twenty-five tractors. The money was not in tractors at the time, even though other companies were working on prototypes. Bill was forced to file for bankruptcy, and the assets for the tractor were sold to the Western Tractor Company in Kansas City.

The real money for Schafer was in tandem discs, and Bill moved to Harper, where his company failed again. From there, he moved production of the discs to Kingman. Bill had many ideas for products over the years, including campers, truck beds and even a golf cart. He was an inventor, if not the best businessman. For many years, he provided good jobs in the south-central region of Kansas. Time and history have shown that the business of agriculture is a fast-moving one and a volatile adventure at best.

Bill was born in Conception, Missouri, on November 28, 1916. He died on November 16, 2004, in Pratt. He first moved to Cunningham, Kansas, and then resided in the Pratt community for the rest of his life.

SEELYE PATENT MEDICINE

Dr. A.B. Seelye was born near Henry, Marshall County, Illinois, on December 20, 1870. The *A* stands for Alfred. He attended Michigan University, Rush Medical College and College of Physicians and Surgeons in Chicago but did not complete his medical education. His parents, John Mason and Ellen Seelye, moved to Kansas, and Alfred joined them there in 1890.

Alfred moved to Abilene, was a lifelong resident and remained active in the community his whole life. In Abilene, he established a small laboratory and engaged in the manufacture of Wasa-Tusa. It was a priority medicine and well received by the public from the start. Other remedies were added until the company offered one hundred different preparations. In 1913, a product called Fro-Zona was added and quickly became a rival for the original Wasa-Tusa.

Plans were made for a new laboratory, which cost $100,000 when completed. The company had been incorporated in 1897 as the A.B. Seelye Medical Company. In 1900, Alfred purchased the Bonebrake Opera House, which was the largest building in town, for $15,000. The west end was the opera house, and the company occupied the rest of the building. The building was sixty by one hundred feet and three stories tall.

All the additional space allowed room for corporate offices, laboratories, shipping, receiving and storerooms. The company employed three hundred local and traveling salesmen, who constituted its sales force. The company also employed skilled technicians and workers. Through the high volume of business, the products manufactured by the company were in thousands of homes all over the central part of the nation. The company had phenomenal growth, and Alfred was very much the spirit of the company.

Alfred invested in large holdings in the Lawton, Oklahoma area and had a residence in Kansas City, as well as the Seelye Mansion in Abilene. He was deeply concerned with the well-being and growth of the Abilene community. He was a member of the Methodist Church, the Sons of the Revolution and was a forty-five-year member of the Masonic Lodge.

When Alfred died on February 14, 1948, he was survived by two daughters and his wife, Jennie Taylor Curts, who was originally from Abilene. They had married in Chicago.

The last daughter of Alfred and Jennie was a lifelong resident of Abilene. She was considered a member of one of the last prominent families in Abilene. The obituary in the *Wichita Eagle* stated that "her life had paralleled the history of Abilene." Helen was ninety-five years old when she passed away. Her sister, Marion, had died in 1988. They told stories of making the patented medicine in her mother's kitchen.

Helen was a staunch Republican, as her father had been, and was a good friend of Alf Landon. Alf's daughter, Nancy Kassebaum, was a United States senator from Kansas. Helen carried on her activities in the community as her father had and was the former director of the Abilene Red Cross and a member of the Daughters of the American Revolution.

TOM FEIST—FEIST PUBLICATIONS

It seems that Kansas farmers come up with a lot of great ideas and have the willpower to pursue a dream and make a business out of it. Tom Feist is another of those people. In the process of creating a company, he built the foundations of a town, providing jobs and opportunities.

Tom was not only a farmer and rancher but also taught in the high school at Spearville from 1959 through 1972. He was also a school board member. He taught his kids that hard work and attention to detail was the most important thing. All through the years at his company, whenever a proposal was written by his employees about company policies and direction, he would use a red pencil and circle the changes he wanted to see made until the proposal was letter perfect. The teacher in him never left.

Tom and his wife decided that there needed to be area-wide telephone directories and that the ones put out by each of the telephone companies did not provide enough coverage. For this reason, they created the Feist Regional Directories. Of course, this drew the ire of the telephone companies, which had a virtual monopoly on directories. A lawsuit was filed, and Tom fought it all the way to the United States Supreme Court. The landmark decision *Feist v. Rural Telephone* went beyond what the intent of the suit was. The decision, with the majority opinion written by Justice O'Connor, cleared up ambiguities in copyright law. This held that factual information was not copyrightable.

Bruce Vierthaler was co-owner of the *Spearville News.* Tom went to him and said that he was getting into business and insisted that he would not do it if Vierthaler did not do the printing. So he did. It was a major undertaking for the small print shop, and the first *Feist Book* came out in the spring of 1978. The new book was not like any directory before and included coupons and maps.

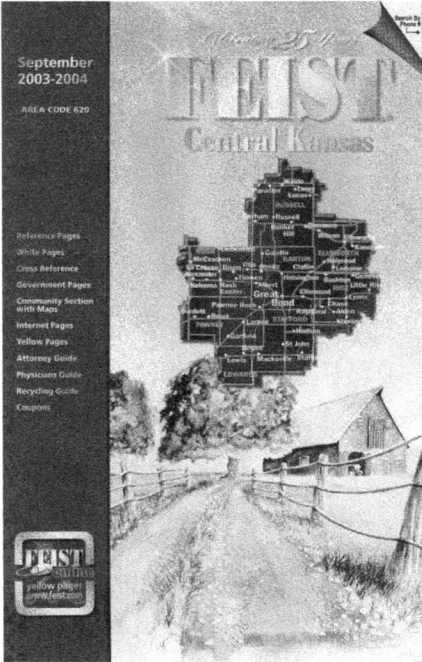

Left: Feist directory. *Courtesy of the Eck Agency.*

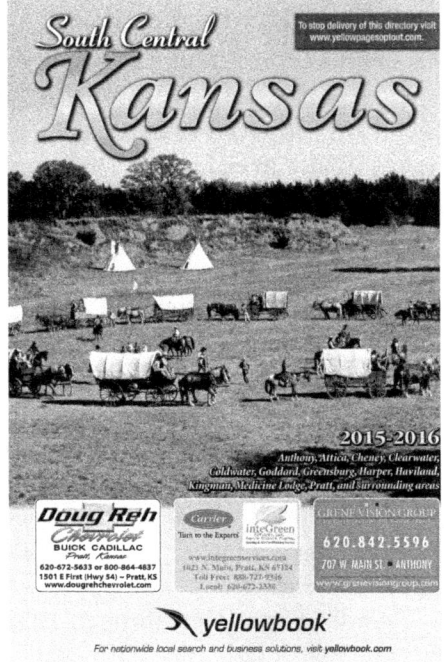

Right: Yellow Book purchased Feist and became nationwide. *Courtesy of the Eck Agency.*

Feist became the fifth-largest directory company in the nation and eventually distributed twenty different regional directories. The sixty jobs that the company created in Spearville made it the third-largest employer in town. It was a major influence in the area. The headquarters were moved to Wichita, but the production stayed in Spearville until the announcement came.

"Yellow Book Buys Out Feist!" In 2004, the announcement came as a shock to the town and employees. A large nationwide directory named Yellow Book had purchased the company. With the acquisition of Feist, Yellow Book expanded into forty-two states with five hundred directories. The announcement ensured that all 599 jobs would remain with Yellow Book.

In 2007, the other shoe dropped, and the announcement was made that production in Spearville would cease. It was a shock. The loss of sixty jobs in an eight-hundred-resident town was a major blow that was felt throughout the region. People working for Yellow Book came from Kinsley and Dodge City as well as the Spearville area. Although there were offers to keep jobs and move to other locations, it is not known how many employees took them up on that offer.

Tom was a majority owner of the Ford County Bank. His management style was easygoing, and he did not believe in micromanaging. Tom had earned a bachelor's degree in education from St. Mary's of the Plains College.

Tom Feist died at age seventy-seven on January 17, 2011. He was a Civil War buff, avid runner, cyclist, landscape photographer and big fan of the Kansas City Royals and Chiefs and the KU Jayhawks. He was a recipient of the Kelsey's Group Lifetime Achievement Award for his innovative leadership in the yellow page industry.

The Feist Directories were created on the table in the family room with his wife and six children. Not an uncommon story in Kansas.

NORTON COUNTY METEORITE

Meteorites are something that Kansas has been famous for over the years. For many years, a large meteorite was on display outside the office of Blasi Oil Company on West Kellogg in Wichita. The meteor was found in an alfalfa field on a relative's farm. For many years, there has been a professional meteorite hunter in the Haviland area who has unearthed some very impressive pieces.

The rarest of the rare is when a meteorite is actually witnessed to fall to earth and recovered. That is the case with the Norton County Meteorite. On February 18, 1948 (16:48 hours), in broad daylight, a meteor came streaking through the sky and fell onto a ranch in Norton County, with pieces also falling in Furnas County, Nebraska.

The event caused quite a stir. It caught the attention of the University of Nebraska and the University of New Mexico at Albuquerque. Soon, Dr. Lincoln La Paz was dispatched to investigate and retrieve the meteor. The two universities bought the major portion of the meteor that weighed 1,070 kilograms, or 2,360 pounds. They also bought a large portion of the fragments that were found in the two counties.

The meteor was named for the place it came down, Norton County, Kansas. The type of meteor is of a rarer aubrite. The availability of the pieces of the meteor are rather expensive since the University of New Mexico owns the largest portion of it, which it has on display. There are a few pieces of the meteor in private holdings. A relative of the landowner has a piece that was appraised on *Antiques Road Show* in 2012 for a value of $5,000 to $7,000.

Dr. Lincoln La Paz was born in Wichita, Kansas, on February 12, 1897. He earned his BA degree from Fairmont College (WSU) and taught there from 1917 to 1920. He earned his master's degree at Harvard in 1922 and taught there for some time. From 1922 to 1925, he taught at Dartmouth. He earned his PhD in 1928 at the University of Chicago, taught there for a short time and acted as a National Research Fellow. In 1930, he became assistant professor at Ohio State University; he eventually became an associate professor and then a full professor. In 1942, he developed the Graduate Mathematics Program at Ohio State.

World War II took him to New Mexico Proving Grounds, where he was a research mathematician and later technical director of operations. He was an analyst for the Second U.S. Air Force. His work included investigating the Japanese Fugo Balloon Bombs. He was associated with the investigation of the Roswell, New Mexico UFO incident of 1947. His investigations into the New Mexico Green Fireballs are most well documented. His name is associated with UFO investigations.

La Paz began an investigation of orbiting earth satellites with fellow astronomer Clyde Tombaugh (a graduate of the University of Kansas known for having discovered Pluto). La Paz was a pioneer in the field of meteorites and established the meteorite program at the University of New Mexico. He established the most outstanding collection of meteorites at UNM.

La Paz was a regular contributor to *Popular Astronomy* and established the *Journal of Meteoritics*. His research produced 120 scientific articles and books.

Lincoln married Leota Ray Butler and had two children, Leota Jean and Mary Strode. He lived to be eighty-eight and died on October 19, 1986, in New Mexico.

LYMAN FRANK BAUM

L. Frank Baum never lived in Kansas. So how does he find his way into this book? Answer: *The Wizard of Oz*, which was his creation and has arguably had a huge impact on the image of Kansas. His writing, long after his death, has created a body of work that tries to portray the Wizard into a political allegory. But we will get to that later.

Who was this non-Kansan who had such an impact? He was born Lyman Frank Baum on May 15, 1856, in Chittenango, New York. He was the son of an affluent family and was the seventh of nine children of Benjamin and Cynthia Ann Stanton Baum. They lived on an expansive estate known as Rose Lawn. Frank considered his boyhood home to be a paradise. He was sickly and a dreamy kid and was tutored at home. For two years, he was sent to a military school, which he described as "two years of Hell!"

Frank started writing early in life, and his father bought him a small printing press. With a younger brother, he published *The Rose Lawn Home Journal*, complete with advertising. By age seventeen, he had published a second journal called *The Stamp Collector*. He started a stamp collecting business with his friends and published a pamphlet called *Baum's Complete Stamp Dealers Directory*. He also became involved with raising and showing fancy poultry, establishing the monthly trade journal *The Poultry Journal*, and published a book on the Hamburg chicken.

Frank's lifetime infatuation was the theater. He performed plays under the stage name of Louis F. Baum and George Brooks. In 1880, his father built him a theater in Richburg, New York. He wrote several plays and had an acting company to perform them. *The Maid of Arran* was a moderate

Wizard of Oz postcard, MGM Grand. *Author's collection.*

success. During this time, he married Maud Gage, the daughter of a famous women's suffragette and activist. The theater caught fire and burned to the ground. Most of his stories and scripts were lost in the fire.

In July 1888, Frank and his wife moved to Aberdeen, South Dakota. They ran a store there but had too liberal a credit policy and were soon bankrupted. He edited the local paper and wrote a column after the death of Sitting Bull calling for the extermination of the Native American people, taking the position that the people would not assimilate with society and were a danger. In later examination of his work, it is thought that his writing on the subject was for the purpose of shocking people and to generate positions favorable to the Native people.

In 1897, Baum published a book called *Father Goose*, a collection of nonsense poetry, which had fair success. In 1900, he published *The Wonderful Wizard of Oz*, which had good critical acclaim, and the first printing of the book—ten thousand copies—sold out in two weeks. He went on to create a musical based on the book, which was rejected. A stage version opened in 1902 with the shortened title *The Wizard of Oz*. Opening in Chicago, it ran on Broadway for 293 stage nights in 1903, returned in 1904 and had a successful road tour.

Baum wanted to write children's stories that did not have the violence and gore that other fairy tales had. With his success, he announced that he had bought an island and was going to create the Marvelous Land of Oz Amusement Park. The project never came to be a reality.

Throughout his life, Frank tried to re-create the success of the first Wizard of Oz book. He produced thirteen books in the Oz series, but none achieved the success of the first. It was the 1939 colorized movie version of *The Wizard of Oz* that created the blockbuster that it still is today. Twenty-five years after Frank's death, a high school history teacher, Henry Littlefield, created the political allegory interpretation of the Wizard. This started a discourse that survives to this day. The time frame in which the story was written was a period of political turmoil with the election of McKinley and rise of Populism. There are debates and college courses on the subject to this day. Although the story was based on his time in South Dakota, Kansas was the backdrop and has been forever linked to the story. Like it or not, the image of Kansas continues to be the tornado and the line "I don't think we are in Kansas anymore, Toto."

TALLEST MAN IN CONGRESS

"Tallest man in Congress" is what the postcard said, and Daniel Read Anthony Jr. does appear to be well over six feet tall. But nowhere in my research can I find how tall he actually was. Daniel was the son of a Kansas patriot and newspaperman, Daniel Read Anthony. His aunt—his father's sister—was Susan B. Anthony of equal rights fame.

Born in Leavenworth, Kansas, on August 22, 1870, Daniel attended public schools and went on to Michigan Military Academy in Orchard Lake, Michigan. He then went to the University of Michigan at Ann Arbor, where he earned a law degree. He was admitted to the bar but did not practice. He came back to Leavenworth to work in the newspaper business. He was then appointed postmaster for Leavenworth, serving in that position from 1898 until 1902. He then became mayor of Leavenworth from 1903 until 1905.

In 1904, he became managing editor of the *Leavenworth Times* newspaper. He was then elected to Congress to fill the First District seat that had been held by Charles Curtis. Curtis moved up to the Senate and later became vice president. Daniel was reelected several times, serving from 1907 until 1929.

One website that rates the performance of elected officeholders cites that Daniel's voting record was lower than his contemporaries. The report says that Daniel missed 45.4 percent of roll call votes. There is no analysis that takes into consideration how travel times and activities affected the ability to vote. There is one thing certain, however. Along with Senator Charles Curtis, Daniel co-sponsored the Equal Rights Amendment to the Constitution. It is fitting that Susan B. Anthony's nephew was co-sponsor of the amendment.

One of the major projects that Daniel was behind was the building of the National Military Road from Fort Leavenworth to Fort Riley. Daniel also served on the board of directors of the Leavenworth National Bank. He married Elizabeth Havens of Leavenworth and had two children, Eleanor and Daniel. He had one brother named Madge.

Daniel returned home after several terms in Congress to his business interests. He died in Leavenworth on August 4, 1931. He is interred in Mount Muncie Cemetery.

CORDELL, KANSAS—TORNADOS HIT THREE YEARS IN A ROW

This story is one that many do not know, but every meteorologist in the country does.

Kansas is known to be in "tornado alley," but the truth is that most people in the state will never see one in their lifetime. Some may see one or two, but few see more than that unless they work in emergency services. But what are the odds of having a tornado hit the same town on the same day, three years in a row? Astronomical!

Take the strange case of Cordell, Kansas. The town in Ellis County had a tornado hit on May 20, 1916, 1917 and 1918. Those who have spent their life in Kansas can recognize the weather that tornados usually hit in. A warm, muggy, unsettled day.

Back then, the tornado was called a cyclone. Residents started to call May 20 Cyclone Day after the town of Cordell was hit twice. But there was no humor left when, on the third year in a row, the town was hit again. Stories of what tornados do cannot be outdone by fiction.

On May 20, 1918, Celesta Glendening wrote for her descendants the story of that day. Her husband was working in the cornfield, and Celesta, who was pregnant at the time, was at home with her two young children. As she went out to get the cows, she noticed clouds gathering in the southwest. A storm soon blew in. Gathering her children, they started to go to the root cellar, but the hail started, and they turned back and stayed in the kitchen. As the house shook, they started to smell dust and damp plaster. She knew that it would get worse, and it did. As the wind blew harder, Celesta and George, her husband, went to get the boys. Max was one and a half years old, and Celesta wrapped him in a quilt. As the house started to rip apart, Max was suddenly pulled from her arms. In a flash of lightning, she saw Max hovering above the floor, sitting up.

George grabbed Max out of the air and handed him back to his mother. They all huddled together until the storm passed. They had cuts and bruises, but they all survived. There were more experiences similar to theirs. Three residents of Cordell died in 1918.

It was reported that every motor car in Hays was used to carry workers to Cordell to help in the recovery. The county coroner had men go down in a milk cellar and tear up floorboards to carry away the bodies of Mr. and Mrs. Geist. It was reported that the bodies of Mr. and Mrs. Geist had been blown into a barbed-wire fence and that they were caked with mud that had been hardened by the pounding hail.

Cletus at memorial. No, it is not Toto. It is Cletus at the memorial for tornado victims. *Courtesy of Joseph Becker.*

The 1918 tornado started fifteen miles northeast of Hays at the McIntosh place and moved through the Geist farm. At that point, the tornado was one mile wide. One-half mile north of the Geist farm was the Adam Geist home, where three children were killed.

Miraculously, the house of George Bahl was picked up and deposited in a wheat field about one-quarter mile away. All four walls blew outward, but the family sat untouched in one room. On the P.J. Deane ranch every building was blown apart, but the family survived in the storm cave.

In all, ten people lost their lives in the 1918 storm.

Joel Russell grew up in Cordell and had heard the stories of the three tornados on the same day three years in a row. Joel and his wife settled back in Cordell. He realized that the centennial of the last tornado event was soon coming up. He called the economic director about an idea to commemorate the event. Director Roger Hrabe thought it was a good idea.

A call was put in to the Dane G. Hansen Foundation about having a memorial made to remember those terrible events. Two Fort Hays State University faculty artists started working on a metal statue and memorial. To raise funds, donors' names were stamped on the steel bands used in the sculpture.

The resulting sculpture is a twelve-foot-tall tornado funnel cloud. At the dedication were two people who had lived through the Cordell tornados: Ellen Hocket, 105, and Lee Smith, 103, her brother.

Newspapers recorded dozens of people's experiences and close calls from the tornados. One clipping was seen tacked to the wall in a Boston tavern a few years ago. The fact that there is not a meteorologist who does not know the story of the Cordell tornados testifies to the unusualness of the facts. Those who study tornados are fascinated by the fact that the same town was hit on the same day, three years in a row.

BIBLIOGRAPHY

Rooks County Tragedy, Four Children Burned

Find a Grave. "Lily May Losey." www.findagrave.com/memorial/113373600/lily-may-losey.

Jewell County Republican. "Children Die in Fire." December 23, 1904, 7.

Kirwin Kansan. "Burned to Death!" December 15, 1904, 1.

Phillipsburg Herald. December 15, 1904, front page.

Stockton Review and Rooks County Record. "Children Die by Fire." December 16, 1904, 1.

www.newspapers.com.

Cottonwood Davis

Altamont Journal. "Cottonwood Davis Dead." January 19, 1911, 2.

Biography of Charles Wood Davis. https://accessgenealogy.com/california/biography-of-charles-wood-davis.htm.

Connelley, William E. *A Standard History of Kansas and Kansans*. Chicago: Lewis Publishing, 1918. 5 vols. "Charles W Davis." www.ksgenweb.org/archives/1918ks/biod/daviscw.html.

Cutler, William G. *History of the State of Kansas, Part 2, Township Sketches*. Kansas Collection Books. 1883. www.kancoll.org/books/cutler/sedgwick/sedgwick-co-p2.html.

Daily Republican (Anthony). "About Railroads." June 17, 1886, 4.

Girard Press. "C. Wood Davis Dead." January 5, 1911, 4.

Harper Daily Sentinel. "Cottonwood Davis to Succeed Prince Alexander." December 15, 1886, 1.

Hutchinson News. "Cottonwood Davis." January 6, 1911, 4.

Meany, Vol. P. *History of Butler County, Kansas*. Lawrence, KS: Standard Publishing Company, 1916, 336.

Salina Daily Union. "Dug First Salt Well in Salina." January 2, 1911, 3.

Sedgwick County, Kansas, County Clerk's Office.

A Twentieth Century History and Biographical Record of Crawford County. Chicago: Lewis Publishing, 1905, 110–17.

Wichita City Eagle. "Frontier Boys Meet after Forty Years." November 11, 1913.

Wichita Daily Eagle. "Must Pay or Appeals." January 8, 1916, 5.

Wichita Weekly Beacon. "Railroad Talk." April 9, 1876, 2.

www.newspapers.com.

Fried Chicken

Chicken Annie's Menu. www.chickenanniesoriginal.com/htdocs/menu.html.

Chicken Mary's Menu. chicken-marys.com/menu/.

"Chicken Mary's Restaurant, Frontenac, Kansas." www.kansasmemories.org/item/457143.

Food Wars [TV show]. "Pittsburg KS Fried Chicken War." Aired March 16, 2010.

Grisolano, Greg. "Food Wars Aims to Settle Fried-Chicken Competition." *Joplin Globe*.

Grout, Pam, *Kansas Curiosities: Quirky Characters, Roadside Oddities & Other Offbeat Stuff*. Guilford, CT: Globe Pequot, 2002.

"The History of Chicken Annie's." www.ckt.net/sites/zagspage/cag/history.htm.

Kansas Sampler Foundation. "8 Wonders of Kansas Cuisine." www.kansassampler.org/8wonders/cuisineresults.php.

Trillin, Calvin. "Fried Chicken War." *New Yorker Magazine*, March 8, 1982, 100.

Jeff Duree—Bank Robber

Arizona Republic. "Man Taken Is Notorious Robber and Bail Jumper." May 9, 1925, 1.

Bartlesville Daily Enterprise. "Jeff Duree Is Wanted in Colorado." August 7, 1920, 3.

Coffeyville Daily Journal. "Raided Auto Thieves." May 22, 1917, 6.

Daily Oklahoman. "Jeff Duree Captured in Arizona." May 9, 1924, 3.

Farris, David. "Last Train Robbery." March 9, 2017. edmondlifeandleisure. com/last-train-robbery-p14251-76.htm.

Find a Grave. "Jeff Duree." www.findagrave.com.

"Jefferson Davis Duree, Grenola's Notorious Gang Leader!" www.grenolaks. com/history.html.

Kansas City Times. "Named in Holdup." August 27, 1958.

Kansas Historical Society. "Jeff Davis Duree." www.kshs.org/ archives/227035.

Kansas Memory. Jeff Duree. www.kansasmemory.org/item.

Moline Advance. "Bandit Slain." August 14, 1924, 1.

Potter, Jim. "A Day I Shall Never Forget." Blog post, October 30, 2019. Sandhenge Publications. jimpotterauthor.com/a-day-i-shall-never-forget/.

St. Louis Post-Dispatch. "Ghost Bandit from 'Up in the Osage' Leads Sleuths a Chase Unique." February 15, 1925, 96.

www.newspapers.com.

Maud Stevens Wagner—Tattoo Artist

Bell, Carley. "Biography: Maud Wagner Stevens—Tattooist." February 14, 2016. www.theheroinecollective.com/maud-wagner/.

Brooks, Ryann. "Notable Women Discussed in Kickoff of New Historical Society Series." *Emporia Gazette*, March 17, 2018.

Find a Grave. "Maud & Gus Wagner." www.findagrave.com.

Giometti, Giulia. "Meet Maud Wagner." www.tattoolife.com/meet-maud-wagner/.

"The Graves of Maud and Gus Wagner." www.atlasobscura.com/places/ the-graves-of-maud-and-gus-wagner.

MacGowan, Douglas. "Maud Stevens and the Rise of the Female Tattoo Artist." Treehugger. June 8, 2015. www.mnn.com/lifestyle/arts-culture/ stories/maud-stevens-and-the-rise-of-the-female-tattoo-artist.

"Maud Stevens Wagner Introduced to Tattoos by Merchant Marine."
   reference.jrank.org/biography-2/Wagner_Maud_Stevens.html.
Star Tribune. "Tattoo." July 20, 2016, E3.

Mrs. Amy Loucks—Lakin

"Charles Allen Loucks." www.ksgenweb.org.
Connelley, William E. *A Standard History of Kansas and Kansans*. Vol. 4. N.p.:
   HardPress Publishing, 2013, 1901.
Find a Grave. "Amy Loucks." www.findagrave.com/memorial/41076869/
   amy-m-loucks.
Kansas State Historical Society.
"Settlement of Southwest Kansas." www.gardencity.net/info/history/
   weskan/.

Octagonal City

Hughes, Alexandra, and Hanna Smith. "Octagon City: A Utopian Society."
   February 16, 2017. prezi.com/4e35vxmn5qfq/octagon-city-a-utopian-
   society.
"Kansas: A Vegetarian Utopia; The Letters of John Milton Hadley 1855–
   1856." *Kansas History: A Journal of the Central Plains* 38, no. 1 (Spring 1972):
   65–87.
The Kansas Herald of Freedom. "Octagon City—Initial Plans." April 28, 1855, 1.
Zhang, Sarah. "When Vegetarians Tried to Build a Utopia of Octagonal
   Houses in Kansas." *Utopia Week*, April 18, 2014.

Walterscheid Brothers Foundry—Automobile Company

All Car Index. www.allcarindex.com/main-index/car-make-details/United-
   States.
American Machinist 23. April 19, 1900, 382–444.
Der Carroll Demokrat (German translation). www.europeanline-magazine.
   eu/wikisearch.php?title=automarket.
Farm Implement News 13, Buyer Guide, January–June 1892 and July–
   December 1892.

The Horseless Age: Automobile Trade Magazine 9 (1902): 154.

The Implement Blue Book: The Standard Implement and Vehicle. St. Louis: Midland Publishing Co., 1909, 262, 264, 271, 273, 290, 293.

The Saturday Evening Kansas Commoner. Advertisement. January 23, 1902, 5.

Wendel, C.H. *Encyclopedia of American Farm Equipment and Antiques.* Iola, WI: Krause Publications, 1977.

Wichita Beacon. "Tihen Notes." Wichita State University Special Collections. August 2, 1902, 4.

————. "Wichita Pump Factory." July 11, 1902, 3.

Wichita Daily Eagle. "Afraid of Automobiles." November 25, 1902.

————. "Automobile Parade at Eleven O'Clock." September 30, 1904, 5.

————. "Autos Built Here." January 19, 1902, 5.

————. "Autos—Three Machines Being Built in Wichita." June 25, 1902, 6.

————. "Only $500." April 26, 1903, 7.

Wichita Star. Advertisement. June 20, 1902, 5.

Winfield Daily Courier. "Will Build Automobiles." January 21, 1902, 4.

Sam and Esther Zelman

"Esther Zelman Moses." www.legacy.com/obituaries/cjonline/obituary. aspx?n=esther-zelman-moses&pid=147940832&fhid=4860.

Finger, Stan. "Store Owner, Auschwitz Survivor Moses Dies." *Wichita Eagle*, January 21, 2011.

Great Plains Quarterly. "Jewish Community in Wichita 1920–1970, Same Wagon, New Horses." (Fall 2008): 293–320.

"My Heritage, Sam Zelman." www.myheritage.com/names/sam_zelman.

Wichita Eagle and Beacon. "Tihen Notes." Wichita State University Special Collections. 1974.

www.Zelemanlofts.com.

Smitty the Jumper

Billum, Thomas D. "Skydiver for 47 Years: 'Smitty the Jumper' Surrounded by Past." *Salina Journal*, May 13, 1976, 6.

Brogdon, Tony. "Smitty the Jumper." www.dropzone.com/forums/topic /55125-smitty-the-jumper/. August 5, 2003.

Flying Magazine. "Smitty the Jumper." 66, no. 5 (May 1960): 8.

Garrity, John. "Things Have a Way of Falling into Place for a Jaunty Octogenarian." *Sports Illustrated*, April 21, 1986.

"Smitty the Jumper." Photo from Burrell Tibbs Collection at the University of Texas at Dallas. Photo published July 22, 2014. utd-ir.tdl.org/handle/10735.1/3757.

Viletto, Moe. "Throwback Thursday—Smitty." *Blue Skies Magazine*, June 19, 2014.

University Farm

KU Student Farm. biosurvey.ku.edu/field-station.

KU Student Farming/Alternative Farming. www.nal.usda.gov/afsic/edtr/ku-student-farm-university-kansas.

Learning Pathways, Food & Agriculture. esp.ku.edu/food-and-agriculture.

Sunflower Journeys. Season 24, Episode 2406, November 2, 2011. watch.opb.org/video/ktwu-sunflower-journey-sunflower-journeys.

University of Kansas Student Farm—What's Growing On? kufarming wordpress.com/.

Ralph Winship—Majestic Theater

Huck Boyd Institute. "Kansas Profiles 2011." www.huckboydinstitute.org/kansas-profiles/profiles/2011.html.

Majestic Community Owned Theater. www.getruralkansas.com/Phillipsburg/118Explore/848.shtml.

Movie Theater of Phillips County. genealogytrails.com/kan/phillips/movietheater.html.

Phillipsburg Drive-In. cinematreasures.org/theaters/48576.

Salina Journal. "Reluctant Theater Owner Retires from 'Show Biz.'" February 2, 1969, 23.

www.newspapers.com.

Neosho Falls

Bridge, Neosho Falls, Woodson County, Kansas. www.kshs.org/index.php?url=km/items/view/444618.

Neosho Falls Explorations. getruralkansas.org/Neosho-Falls/174Explore/864. shtml.

Neosho Falls from a Different Perspective. www.kansassampler.org/erv/blog.php?act=view&id=41.

Neosho Falls—Ghost Town. www.ghosttowns.com/states/ks/neoshofalls. html.

Neosho Falls Waterfall. www.kansastravel.org/neoshofalls.htm.

Wiser, Kathy. "Neosho Falls." Updated March 2017. www.legendsofkansas. com/neoshofalls.html.

Kansas Highway Patrol

Kansas Highway Patrol. Kansapedia. Kansas Historical Society. www.kshs.org.

Kansas Highway Patrol Official Website. www.kansashighwaypatrol.org/.

Officer Down Memorial Page. www.odmp.org/.

Kansas Pack Goats—Dwite and Mary Sharp

Dybedahl, Jake. "Paradise Ranch Pack Goats." *Sportsman's Guide*, November 12, 2014.

Emporia Gazette. "Packgoats Take Stage." October 10, 2013.

Farm Show Magazine. "Sharp's Pack Goats Bred to Carry." 2015. Vol. 39, no. 6, 8.

Free Standing Displays. Kansas Sampler. www.kansassampler.org/page. php?id=552.

Goat Tracks Magazine; Journal of the Working Goat. "Paradise Ranch Packgoats: For Sale! Dwite Sharp, Council Grove, Kansas." Summer 2016.

Marc Warnke Podcast. "Dwite Sharp." packgoats.com/pack-goat-podcast-45/.

Paradise Ranch Adventures. www.travelks.com/listing/paradise-ranch-adventures-llc/5409/.

Rumbaugh, Shauna. "No Kidding: Pack Goats Are Premier Pack Animals." *High Plains Journal*, August 29, 2016.

Tanner, Beccy. "Kansas Sampler Festival Celebrates—Kansas." *Wichita Eagle*, April 26, 2015.

Henry's Candy

Author's recollections.

Get Rural Kansas. "Henry's Candy Company." www.getruralkansas.com/ Dexter/57index.shtml.

Grout, Pam. *Kansas Curiosities: Quirky Characters, Roadside Oddities & Other Offbeat Stuff.* Guilford, CT: Globe Pequot, 2002.

Henry's Candy Company. kansastransportation.blogspot.com/2016/08/ motoring-monday-henrys-candy-company.html.

History of the Williamson Candy Co. and Oh Henry. www. madeinchicagomuseum.com/single-post/williamson-candy-co.

Only in Your State. "The Delightful Candy Company That's Been Hiding in Small Town Kansas for 60 Years." www.onlyinyourstate.com/kansas/ ks-candy-company/. November 5, 2018.

Loyd Ratts—Farmer, Inventor, Centenarian

Griekspoor, P.J. "Meet Loyd Ratts, a 'Century Farmer' Who Has Lived Every Minute to the Max." *Kansas Farmer*, July 21, 2016.

Gullichson. Gil. "SF Special: Kansas Farmer Still Going Strong at 102." *Successful Farming*, June 20, 2017.

Hoener, Chance. "The Many Lives of Loyd Ratts." *Hutchinson News*, February 27, 2018.

Hutchinson News. Loyd E. Ratts. Obituary. November 30, 2018.

Rose, Gail. "Loyd Ratts Turns 103." *St. John News*, February 14, 2018.

Spradly, Terry. "St. John Farmer Invents System to End the Climb." *Pratt Tribune*, January 15, 2014.

Karrin Allyson—Jazz Great

Brownlee, Bill. "Karrin at The Folly Theater." *Kansas City Star*, December 20, 2014.

Holden, Stephen. "A Sharp Eye for Songs in the Key of Now." *New York Times*, June 3, 2011.

Karrin Allyson. "Biography." karrin.com/wp-content/uploads/2019/02/ Karrin-Bio-Final.pdf.

My Music Base. "Biography—Karrin Alyson." October 14, 2016. www. mymusicbase.ru/PPB/ppb8/Bio_842.htm.

NPR. "Karrin Allyson Sings for Kansas City." July 24, 2008. www.npr.org/artists/15328581/karrin-allyson.

Thacker, Susan. "Karrin Allyson Coming to Jazz Festival." *Great Bend Tribune*, November 27, 2018.

Dixie Lee—Madam

Find a Grave. "Inez A. 'Dixie Lee' Griffing Oppenheimer." www.findagrave.com/memorial/75729109/inez-a-Oppenheimer.

Genealogy & Family Tree. Oppenheimer 1800s. www.onegreatfamily.com.

"Inez A. 'Dixie Lee' Griffing Oppenheimer Biography." www.griffingweb.com/inez_griffing,_part_2.htm.

Kansas City Journal. "Evidently Demented." December 14, 1896, 2.

King and Queen of Cowtown. www.oldcowtown.org/VB/Pages/2017-10-05.aspx.

Oppenheimer, Dixie Lee. *Wichita Eagle* and *Wichita Beacon.* "Tihen Notes." Wichita State University Special Collections. specialcollections.wichita.edu/collections/local_history/tihen/pdf/People&Places/Dixie_Lee.pdf. 1894–1901.

Passengers Arrived in Style. www.historicpreservationalliance.com/WichitaHPA/MissouriPacific.html.

San Francisco Call. "Inherits the Wealth of Mrs. Oppenheimer." February 8, 1901, 9.

Sedgwick County, Kansas—Geneology Trails. ww1.geneologytrails.com/kan/sedgwick/newspapertidbitsindex.htm.

Stumpe, Joe. *Wicked Wichita.* Charleston, SC: The History Press, 2018.

Tanner, Beccy. "1881–1890 Timeline." *Wichita Eagle,* January 29, 2011. www.kansas.com/news/special-reports/kansas-105/article1056256.html.

Wichita Beacon. "Almost Murder." August 16, 1892, 1.

———. "Dixie Dances." March 27, 1895.

———. "Somewhat Rattled." December 15, 1896, 1.

———. "Wrecked His Life." March 4, 1897, 5.

Wichita Daily Eagle. "A Big Damage Suit." August 27, 1890, 5.

———. "Blocks Depot Deal." January 30, 1900.

———. "Comes Down Hard." December 20, 1896, 5.

———. "He Died in Prison." March 4, 1897, 5.

Wichita Then and Now. www.wichitavortex.com/ict/036.html.

Wichita Weekly Beacon. "That Oppenheimer Case." October 2, 1891, 4.

Nannie Jones

Arnold, Ashley. "Long Forgotten Story Remembered Through Memorial." www.ksn.com/news/long-forgotten-story-remembered-through-memorial/.

Campney, Brent M.S. *This Is Not Dixie: Racist Violence in Kansas, 1861–1972.* Champaign: University of Illinois Press, 2015.

Stumpe, Joe. "Neighbors West." *Wichita Eagle*, March 16, 2016.

———. *Wicked Wichita*. Charleston, SC: The History Press, 2018.

Tanner, Beccy. "Righting a Wrong, Wichitans Gather to Honor Nannie Jones." *Wichita Eagle*, July 20, 2016.

Wichita Beacon. "Jury Awards Colored Woman." "Tihen Notes." February 20, 1909, 5. Wichita State University Special Collections. specialcollections.wichita.edu/collections/local_history/tihen/pdf/beacon/Beac1909.pdf.

Cross Manufacturing

Cross Manufacturing Company. "Cross History." crossmfg.com/about/history.

Great Bend Tribune. "The Cross Mfg. of Lewis Proves Industry and Small Towns Go Well Together." June 23, 1966, 1.

———. "Manufacturing Plant to Locate in Pratt." June 18, 1953, 5.

———. "New Industry for Kinsley." September 2, 1960, 2.

Hays Daily News. "Kinsley Plant Closing." September 20, 1971, 1.

———. "Plant Transitions Completed." December 6, 1971, 1.

———. "Welcome Again to Cross." September 21, 1971, 4.

Kansas Historical Society. "Cross Manufacturing Company." www.kshs.org/archives/450384.

Salina Journal. "Authorize Revenue Bonds for Hays Plant." March 13, 1970.

Buddy Rogers—Olathe

American Experience. www.pbs.org/wgbh/americanexperience/features/pickford-buddy-roger-mary-pickford-and-their-children.

Find a Grave. "Buddy Rogers." www.findagrave.com/memorial/5413/buddy-rogers.

Golden Silents. "Charles 'Buddy' Rogers." www.goldensilents.com/stars/charlesbuddyrogers.html.

IMDb. "Charles 'Buddy' Rogers Biography." www.imdb.com/name/nm0736777/.

Johnson, Richard J., and Bernard Henry Shirley, comps. *American Dance Bands on Record and Film, 1915–1942*. N.p.: Rustbooks Publishers, 2010.

Kansapedia. "Charles 'Buddy' Rogers." www.kshs.org/kansapedia/charles-buddy-rogers/18143.

Oliver, Myrna. "From the Archives: Buddy Rogers, Star of Silent Era, Husband of Mary Pickford Dies." *Los Angeles Times*, April 22, 1999.

Van Guilder, Lawrence. "Buddy Rogers, Star of Wings and Band Leader, Dies at 94." *New York Times*, April 23, 1999.

David Dary—Historian

Boot Hill Museum. "David Dary—Cowboy Historian." www.boothill.org/david-dary-cowboy-historian/.

Clark, Darrington. "Award Winning Writer Discusses Importance of Small Community Journalism. *Kansas State Collegian*, September 20, 2012. www.kstatecollegian.com/2012/09/20/award-winning-writer-discusses-importance-of-small-community-journalism/.

Goodreads. "Books by David Dary." www.Goodreads.com.

Kansas State University. "David Dary Papers 1856–2013." www.lib.k-state.edu/apps/findingaids/index.php?p=collections/findingaid&id=91&q=&rootcontentid=11102.

Manhattan Mercury. "Manhattan Native David Dary Dies at 83." March 21, 2018.

The Oklahoman. "Former OU Professor, Accomplished Journalist David Dary, Former OU Professor, Distinguished Western Writer, Dies at 83." March 20, 2018.

Publishers Weekly. "Books by David Dary." www.publishersweekly.com/pw/authorpage/david-dary.html.

Random House. "David Dary." www.penguinrandomhouse.com/authors/6427/david-dary.

Tanner, Beccy. "Kansan David Dary, Who Told Great Western Stories, Dies at 83." *Wichita Eagle*, March 20, 2018.

Captain Donald K. Ross, Beverly—Medal of Honor

Emporia Weekly Gazette. "Nearly 8000 See the Freedom Train." June 3, 1948.

Find a Grave. "Capt. Donald K Ross." www.findagrave.com/memorial/8024329/donald-k-ross.

Genealogy Trails. "Medal of Honor Recipients from World War 2 Attack on Pearl Harbor." genealogytrails.com/ww2/PearlHarborMedalofHonor-pg02.html.

Halloran, Richard. "50 Years Later the Nation Remembers." (*New York Times*, UPI). *Manhattan Mercury*, November 10, 1991, 48.

Kansapedia. "Donald K. Ross." www.kshs.org/kansapedia/donald-k-ross/16880.

KVSV Radio. "Gov. Signs Bill Honoring Lincoln County Veteran." www.kvsvradio.com/?page=story&id=500. Accessed January 15, 2020.

Lincoln County Communities. "Beverly." www.livelincolncounty.com/beverly/.

Los Angeles Times. "Donald K. Ross; Winner of Medal of Honor." June 5, 1992.

Manhattan Mercury. "Donald K. Ross." June 2, 1992, 13.

National Archives Catalog. "Captain Donald Kirby Ross, USN Ret." catalog.archives.gov/id/6476466.

New York Times. "Capt. Donald K. Ross 81; Won Medal of Honor." June 1, 1992, B10.

Salina Journal. "Medal of Honor to Beverly Man." May 5, 1952, 11.

———. "Was Pearl Harbor Hero." April 27, 1980.

Vachon, Deane A., PhD. www.hawaiireporter.com/pearl-harbor-first-medal-of-honor-captain-donald-kirby-ross-u-s-navy.

Wichita Eagle. "Highway Named After Medal of Honor Recipient." 2014. www.kansas.com?news/politics-government/article1058201.

Clementine Paddleford

Alexander, Kelly, and Cynthia Harris. *Hometown Appetites*. New York: Gotham Books–Penguin Group, 2009.

Apple, R.W., Jr. New York Times News Service. "Rediscovering Culinary Pioneer Clementine Paddleford." *Chicago Tribune*, August 2, 2006.

Cincinnati Enquirer. "How America Eats." June 26, 1949, 146.

Cyber Civics. "Clementine Paddleford." www.civics.ks.gov/kansas/kansans/journalism.html.

Kansapedia, People. "Clementine Paddleford." www.kshs.org/kansapedia/clementine-paddleford/12162.

McRobbie, Linda Rodriguez. "Clementine Paddleford: Bad Ass Lady Pilot Who Revolutionized the Art of Food Writing." *Mental Floss*, November 1, 2015.

New York Times. "Clementine Paddleford Is Dead; Food Editor of *Herald Tribune*." November 14, 1967.

Saturday Evening Post. "Clementine Paddleford: Her Passion Is Food." April 30, 1949, 43, 56–58. Kansas State University Libraries, University Archives and Manuscripts.

Big Chief Manufacturing—Clinton John Krehbiel

Hutchinson News. "Charter to Big Chief." May 10, 1951, 23.

———. "Consumer Cooperative Buys Big Chief." May 1, 1959, 1, 4.

———. "Let Big Chief Steel Buildings." September 18, 1949, 33.

Hutchinson News Herald Archives. Advertisement. September 17, 1950, 20.

———. "Big Chief Firm Finds It Has Growing Pains." February 22, 1953, 22.

Oklahoma Union Farmer. "Versatile All-Steel Shed." May 1, 1954, 13. www.newspapers.com.

Cobalt Boats

Boating Industry. "Paxson St. Clair Steps Down as Cobalt President, Malibu Board Member." boatingindustry.com/tag/shane-stanfill/.

Boating Magazine. "Malibu Buys Cobalt." June 29, 2017.

Cobalt Boats. www.cobaltboats.com.

Grossman, John. "Location, Location, Location." *Inc. Magazine*, August 1, 2004.

Grout, Pam. "Cobalt Boats." American Profile. May 31, 2011. americanprofile.com/articles/cobalt-boats-kansas-made/.

Kansas Sampler 8 Wonders of Commerce. "Cobalt Boats, Neodesha." www.kansassampler.org/8wonders/commerceresults.php?id=140.

Stanfill, Shane. "Cobalt Boats." www.legendarymarine.com/home/.

Voorhis, Dan [AP]. "Cobalt Boats Stay Afloat in Rough Economy." *Manufacturing Net*, January 25, 2008. www.manufacturing.net/supply-chain/news/13065714/cobalt-boats-stays-afloat-in-rough-economy.

Dixon ZTR

Dixon Industries, Inc. www.dixon-ztr.com.

Journal and Courier (Lafayette, IN). "We've Been Around." May 6, 2003, 5.

Parsons Sun. Advertisement. November 12, 1973, 5.

Wartgow, Gregg. "Husqvarna Terminates Dixon Brand Lawnmowers." September 26, 2014. www.greenindustrypros.com/mowing-maintenance /mowing/article/11703418/dealers-react-to-husqvarnas-decision-to-terminate-dixon-brand.

Funk Brothers

Akron Beacon Journal. "Funks Finance Drive Pressed." March 25, 1939, 1.

Antique Tractor Blog. "Muscle Up Your Classic Ford Tractor." August 10, 2015. antiquetractorblog.com/tag/funk-manufacturing/.

Burner, Fred. "The Ford/Funk Story." Yesterday's Tractors. www. yesterdaystractors.com.

Coffeyville Aviation Heritage Museum. www.kansastravel.org/coffeyville aviationheritagemuseum.htm.

Davisson, Budd. "We Fly the Funkiest (Did We Actually Say That) Classic Around." www.airbum.com/pireps/PirepFunk.html, from *Air Progress.* November 1990.

Eye on Kansas. "Joe and Howard Funk." www.eyeonkansas.org/seast/ montgomery/0703tractorconversions.html.

General Aviation News. "Aviation Pioneer Joe Funk Dies at 94." December 24, 2004. generalaviationnews.com/2004/12/24/aviation-pioneer-joe-funk-dies-at-94/.

McNessor, Mike. "Funk Conversion Brought Power to the People." Hemmings. com blog. August 4, 2017. www.hemmings.com/blog/2017/08/04/funk-conversion-brought-power-to-the-people/.

Sargent, Sparky Barnes. "The New Funk on the Field." *Vintage Airplane,* October 2011. Accessed from eaavintage.org/wp-content/uploads/2013/01/2011-Vol.-39-No.-10-The-_New_-Funk-on-the-Field.pdf.

Sherrod, Pamela. "Deere to Acquire Maker of Original Equipment." *Chicago Tribune,* May 19, 1989, 40.

The Story Behind the Funk Manufacturing Company (8N Conversion). www. ntractorclub.com/eds_stuff/fordtractors/AccessoryInfo/FunkConversions/ The Story Behind the Funk Manufacturing Company.doc.

Harold Bell Wright

Caldwell, Bill. "Shepherd of the Hills Author Harold Bell Wright." *Joplin Globe*, May 19, 2018. www.joplinglobe.com/news/local_news/bill-caldwell-shepherd-of-the-hills-author-harold-bell-wright/article_aa80a119-6da8-5f11-bd20-7e33ef6e1fb9.html.

Facebook. "Harold Bell Wright Branson Museum." April 26, 2019. www.facebook.com/HaroldBellWrightBransonMuseum/posts/while-at-pittsburg-kansas-harold-bell-wright-hbw-married-frances-e-long-they-had/2702498883100710/.

Kansapedia. "Crawford County, Kansas." www.kshs.org/kansapedia/crawford-county-kansas/15274.

New York Times. "Why Is Harold Bell Wright?—Answered by Himself." August 28, 1921, 61.

Pittsburg Daily Headlight. References to Harold Bell Wright (1872–1944) in the *Pittsburg Daily Headlight* compiled by Gene Degruson, 1976.

Lieutenant JG James Allen Maxwell—Goddard

Alabama Journal. "Plane Crashes Kill Four Men." October 15, 1958, 1.

Birmingham News. "Four Navy Men Killed in Fiery Plane Crashes." October 15, 1958, 24.

Central New Jersey News. "Metuchen Flier Killed in Crash." October 15, 1958, 1.

Cheney Sentinel. Family clipping, n.d.

Corsicana Daily Sun. "Four Pilots Lost Tuesday." October 16, 1958, 27.

Department of the Navy. Navy Personnel Command.

The Maxwell family, personal recollections.

National Archives Personnel Records Center.

The News (Paterson, NJ). "4 Navy Fliers Killed in Crashes." October 16, 1958, 41.

Salina Journal. "Kansas Flier Among 3 Killed." October 15, 1958, 21.

McPherson Wetlands

Kansas Department of Wildlife, Parks & Tourism. "McPherson Valley Wetlands Wildlife Area." ksoutdoors.com/KDWPT-Info/Locations/Wildlife-Areas/South-Central/McPherson-Valley-Wetlands.

Queal, Leland. Documents.

Schrag, Rynnell R. "Draining the Big Basin." 1991.

Ernest Dittemore—Doniphan County

Brown, Tony. "This Home Really Is a Hole in the Ground." *Chicago Tribune*, December 1, 1987.

Deseret News. "Kansan Likes His New Life Down Under." February 28, 1993.

Facebook. "Ernest William Dittemore." www.facebook.com/Ernest-William-Dittemore-200860356633002/

Find a Grave. "Ernest William Dittemore." www.findagrave.com/memorial /28157837/ernest-william-dittemore.

McCoy, Daniel. "One of Larry Hatteburg's Most Memorable People." *Wichita Business Journal*, November 13, 2014.

People Staff. "Ernest Dittemore Built a Home and Really Put Himself in a Hole." *People* 29, no. 51, February 28, 1988.

Tulsa World. "Kansan Prefers Life in a Hole to Trailer." March 7, 1993.

Wills, Kendall J. "Farmer Calls Hole His Home—He's the 'Cave Man of Doniphan County.'" *Seattle Times*, March 7, 1993.

Almon Strowger—Automatic Telephone Exchange

About Almon Strowger's Later Life. www.almonbrownstrowger.com/ almon-brown-strowger-later-life/.

Altoona (PA) *Tribune*. "Dial Telephone Invention Traced to Wrath of Wearied Subscriber." December 31, 1928, 7.

Butler County Historical Society.

Carlson, Anna. "Lindsborg Men Invent Dial Telephones in 1883." *Salina Journal*, August 28, 1957, 11.

Council Grove Republican. "Dedicated Telephone Switching System." July 2, 1976, 1.

Doohan, John J. "Kansas Citians Balky Telephone." *Kansas City Times*, December 14, 1955, 42.

Find a Grave. "Almon Brown Strowger." www.findagrave.com/memorial /6892494/almon-brown-strowger.

Hill, R.B. "The Early Years of the Strowger System." *Bell Laboratories Record*, March 1953, 95–103.

Kansapedia. "Almon Strowger." www.kshs.org/kansapedia/almon-strowger/16911.

National Inventors Hall of Fame. "Almon Brown Strowger." Inducted 2006. www.invent.org/inductees/almon-brown-strowger.

Russell Record. "A Kansas Invention." November 5, 1891, 3.

South Bend Tribune. "First Exchange." January 12, 1968, 85.

Spark Museum. "Almon B. Strowger: The Undertaker Who Revolutionized Telephone Technology." www.sparkmuseum.org/almon-b-strowger-the-undertaker-who-revolutionized-telephone-technology/.

www.newspapers.com.

www.telephonetribute.com/switches.html.

Dane Hansen

Dane G. Hansen Foundation. danehansenfoundation.org/.

Dane G. Hansen Memorial Museum. www.kansastravel.org/hansenmuseum.htm.

Dane Hansen Foundation Community Grants. gscf.org/dane-g-hansen-foundation-community-grants/.

Discover Logan. discoverlogan.com/visitors/points-of-interest/.

Hansen Family History and Legacy. hansenmuseum.org/hansen-family/.

Kansapedia. "Dane Hansen." www.kshs.org/kansapedia/dane-hansen/18163.

Rural Kansas Tourism. "Logan Explorations: Dane Gray Hansen." www.getruralkansas.com/Logan/113Explore/810.shtml.

Wilson, Ron. "Kansas Profile—Now That's Rural." Huck Boyd Institute for Rural Development, Kansas State University. www.ksre.k-state.edu/news/stories/.

Edward L. Wirt

American Herford Record and Herd Book, 1911. Vol. 37, 18, 588. hdl.handle.net/2027/uc1.b3243709.

American Kennel Club Stud Book, January to December 1890. Vol. 7, 229.

Daily Sentinel. "The Council." March 22, 1887, 1.

Evening Telegram (Garden City). "Griggs-Wirt Wedding." September 15, 1911, 1.

———. "The Santa Fe Trail Is Properly Marked." September 9, 1909, 1.

Finney County Democrat. "Democratic Ticket." October 22, 1887, 4.

Finney County Historical Society. www.finneycounty.org/170/Historical-Museum.

Garden City Herald. "Ordinance No. 168." February 24, 1910, 7.

Kansas History Project—Finney County Directories. sites.rootsweb.com/~ksfinnhp/directories/directories.html. Website created March 17, 2012.

Kansas State History. "The Garden City Sugar Company." www.kspatriot.org/index.php/articles/34-kansas-commerce/558-the-garden-city-sugar-company.html.

Michael C. Hornung—Crust Buster

Bickle, Amy, Kansas Agland. "Cutting Edge Technology the Focus for Longtime Crust Buster Company." *Hutchinson News*, September 25, 2015.

———. "From Folding Basketball Goals to Folding Drills." *Salina Journal*, September 26, 2015.

Great Bend Tribune. "American Products Foresees Big Year." April 18, 1966, 65.

———. "Spearville's American Products Inc. Is Home-Town Industry." September 13, 1967.

The History of CrustBuster/Speed King, Inc. www.crustbuster.com/the-history-of-crustbuster-speed-king-inc.

Southwest Kansas Register. "Community Foundation of Southwest Kansas." May 6, 2012, 13.

Morganville and Feves, France: Sister Cities

Biles, Jan. "Small Kansas Town Helped French Village Recover from WWII." *Topeka Capital Journal*, November 30, 2013.

Clay Center Dispatch. "K-State Journalism Class Helps Reconnect Towns in Kansas." December 16, 2013.

Clay County, Kansas/Morganville. www.claycountykansas.org/262/Morganville.

Ehrlich, Matthew C. *Radio Utopia: Postwar Audio Documentary in the Public Interest.* Champaign: University of Illinois Press, 2017.

Garcia, Rafael. "French Group Visits Campus." *The* (K-State) *Collegian*, September 10, 2015.

K-State News. "Journalism Class Research Project Linking Morganville to Fèves, France, Results in Special Trip." www.k-state.edu/media/newsreleases/2016-11/feves11116.html.

Parr, Ann. "Thanksgiving and Feves." December 4, 2013. www.annparrwriter.com/blog-1/2013/12/4/thanksgiving-and-feves.

Update (The A.Q. Miller School of Journalism and Mass Communications Alumni Magazine). "A French Village, a Kansas Town: A Historic Connection." Winter 2015–16. jmc.k-state.edu/alumni-friends/update/Update-2015-12.pdf.

Wilson, Ron. "Kansas Profile—Now that's Rural." Huck Boyd Institute for Rural Development, Kansas State University. www.ksre.k-state.edu/news/stories/.

Peggy Hull

Abilene Daily Chronicle. "Only Girl Correspondent." April 8, 1920, 4.

Cyber Civics. "Peggy Hull Deuell." www.civics.ks.gov/kansas/kansans/journalism.html.

Encyclopedia.com. "Peggy Hull." www.encyclopedia.com/women/encyclopedias-almanacs-transcripts-and-maps/hull-peggy-1889-1967.

Geary County Historical Society blog, Catch up on Geary County History. "Petty Hull War Correspondent Started Her Career at the *Junction City Tribune*." March 2014. gearyhistory.blogspot.com/2014/03/peggy-hull-war-correspondent-started.html.

Kansans of the Great War Era. "Peggy Hull." www.kansasww1.org>kansans-of-the-great-war-era-peggy-hull.

Kansapedia. "Peggy Hull." www.kshs.org/kansapedia/peggy-hull-deuell/15137.

Peggy Hull: Her Voice from the Front. www.sites.google.com/site/nationalhistorydaypeggyhull/Home/early-biography.

Peggy Hull Deuell Collection, RH MS 130, Kenneth Spencer Research Library, University of Kansas Libraries. hdl.handle.net/10407/3310580224.

Smith, Wilda M., and Eleanor A. Bogart. *The Wars of Peggy Hull: The Life and Times of a War Correspondent*. El Paso: Texas Western Press, 1991.

President Theodore Roosevelt

Allen County Historical Society. Speech by President Roosevelt [mentioning Funston], Manhattan, Kansas, May 2, 1903. allencountyhistory.weebly. com/speech-by-president-theodore-roosevelt-mentioning-funston.html.

Elliott, David. "President Theodore Roosevelt Presented a Speech in Russell 112 Years Ago Saturday." KRSL, Local News. April 29, 2015. www.krsl. com/local-news/4931-president-theodore-roosevelt-presented-a-speech-in-russell-112-years-ago-saturday.

————. "President Theodore Roosevelt Presidential Speech in Russell." Theodore Roosevelt Center. May 2, 1903. www.theodorerooseveltcenter. org/Research/Digital-Library/Record.aspx?libID=o289773.

Journal Tribune (Knoxville, TN). "Theodore Roosevelt in Kansas City." August 25, 1913, 1.

Kansas Memory. "President Theodore Roosevelt at Manhattan [photo]." May 2, 1903. www.kshs.org/index.php?url=km/items/view/24753.

————. "President Theodore Roosevelt at Osawatomie, Kansas [photo]." August 30, 1910. www.kansasmemory.org/item/676.

LaForte, Robert S. *Kansas Historical Quarterly.* "Theodore Roosevelt's Osawatomie Speech." Vol. 32, no. 2 (Summer 1900): 187–200.

Pearce, Jayne. "The Great Sabbath Day." www.sharonspringsumc.org/ TheGreatSabbathDay.

Rogers, Lisa Waller. "Teddy Roosevelt's Badger." Lisa's History Room. May 14, 2009. lisawallerrogers.com/2009/05/14/teddy-roosevelts-badger/.

————. "Wild Scramble: The White House of Teddy Roosevelt." Lisa's History Room. May 14, 2009. lisawallerrogers.com/2009/05/14/wild-scramble-the-white-house-of-teddy-roosevelt/.

Tanner, Beccy. "Pet Kansas Badger Once Roamed White House." *Wichita Eagle,* September 10, 2012.

Theodore Roosevelt Center. Speech of President Theodore Roosevelt at Abilene, Kansas, May 2, 1903. www.theodorerooseveltcenter.org/ Research/Digital-Library/Record?libID=o289769.

Wichita Beacon. "Col. Roosevelt Spoke to 23,000 Persons in Wichita." April 20, 1912, 1.

Wichita Daily Eagle. "A Real Preparedness." May 31, 1916, 4. www.newspapers.com.

Rory Lee Feek

Blankenship, Bill. "Success Story Has Kansas Roots." *Topeka Capital Journal*, March 18, 2010.

The Boot. "Joey + Rory Feek—Country's Greatest Love Stories." theboot.com/joey-feek-rory-feek-country-love-stories/.

Feek, Rory. "The Amazing Way Rory Feek Sent His Daughter Off to School…Inspired by Joey." *Today* [TV show], October 1, 2018.

———. This Life I Live. www.roryfeek.com/.

Grand Ole Opry. "Rory Feek." www.opry.com/artists/rory-feek/.

Hermanson, Wendy. "Rory Feek Emotional; Life Blog Is Becoming a TV Show." Taste of Country, September 9, 2019. www.tasteofcountry.com/rory-feek-new-series/.

IMDb. "Rory Feek." www.imdb.com/name/nm3020655/.

Singing News. "Rory Feek Hired by RFD TV and Planning a New Weekly Series." www.singingnews.com/news/rory-feek-hired-rfd-tv-new-program/.

Watts, Cindy. "Joey Feek Honored with Funeral, Memorial Service." *The Tennessean*, March 15, 2016, A-2.

Randy Schlitter—RANS Designs

Bergqvist, Pia. "Rans Aircraft Announces Two-Seat Outbound." *Flying Magazine*, July 21, 2016.

Clarkin, Mary. "Sky's the Limit." *Hays Daily News*, November 28, 1989, 15.

8 Wonders of Kansas Commerce Finalist. "Rans Inc., Hays." www.kansassampler.org/8wonders/commerceresults.php?id=134.

Gasper-O'Brien, Diane. "Safety Is Paramount, Says Local Plane Manufacturer." *Hays Daily News*, June 8, 2003, 1.

Johnson, Dan. "35 Years and Counting at Rans Aircraft." generalaviationnews.com. March 29, 2018. generalaviationnews.com/2018/03/29/35-years-and-counting-at-rans-aircraft/.

RANS Aircraft. www.rans.com.

St. Joseph News-Gazette. "Small Town Plane Company Takes Off." November 27, 1989, 11.

Wilson, Ron. Huck Boyd Center for Rural Studies. www.huckboydinstitute.org/.

Wes Jackson—The Land Institute

Bart, Brian. "A Modern Farmer Conversation: The Wisdom of Wes Jackson, Founder of The Land Institute." *Modern Farmer*, March 3, 2017. modernfarmer.com/2017/03/wes-jackson-the-land-institute-kernza/.

Hazzard, Emily Q. "A Conversation with Wes Jackson, President of The Land Institute." *The Atlantic*, March 23, 2011.

The Land Institute. landinstitute.org/.

Lorenz, Jonna. "Distinguished Kansan Wes Jackson: Land Institute Founder Creates First Perennial Grain." *Topeka Capital Journal*, December 29, 2018.

Mead, James R. *Hunting and Trading on the Great Plains, 1859–1875*. Norman: University of Oklahoma Press, 1986.

The Right Livelihood Foundation. "Wes Jackson/The Land Institute." www.rightlivelihoodaward.org/laureates/wes-jackson-the-land-institute/.

William G. Schafer—Schafer Plow Company

Annual Report by the U.S. Patent Office, 1906, 423.

Find a Grave. "William G. Shafer." www.findagrave.com/memorial/920088/william-g-schafer.

Great Bend Tribune. "Sportsman's Truck Body Is New Job." June 9, 1959, 3.

Hutchinson News. "Cotton Harvest Machine Made." November 17, 1950, 21.

Index of patents issued from the United States Patent Office, 1931, 708. U.S. Patent Office, Washington, 1932.

Pratt County Historical Museum. www.prattcountymuseum.org/.

Purple Wave Auction. "1964 Schafer PS 154 tractor." www.purplewave.com/auction/090507/item/3106/Ag_Tractor-Tractor-Kansas.

Rose, Gail. "Prattan Reminisces about Work at Shafer Plow." *Pratt Tribune*, September 20, 2014.

———. "Texas Teen Wins Restoration Contest with Schafer Tractor." *Butler County Times-Gazette*, November 6, 2014.

www.newspapers.com.

Seelye Patent Medicine

8 Wonders of Kansas Architecture. "Seelye Mansion—Abilene." www.kansassampler.org/8wonders/architectureresults.php?id=52.

Enterprise Eagle, February 22, 1900, 5.

Find a Grave. "Alfred Barns Seelye." www.findagrave.com/memorial/38918629/alfred-barns-seelye.

Grout, Pam. *Kansas Curiosities: Quirky Characters, Roadside Oddities & Other Offbeat Stuff*. Guilford, CT: Globe Pequot, 2002.

Kansapedia. "Patent Medicines." www.kshs.org/kansapedia/patent-medicines/12165.

Kansas Memory. "Medicine Bottle." www.kansasmemory.org/item/318744.

Kansas Weekly Capital, June 28, 1901, 3.

Linda's Backroad Musing. "Seelye's Wasa Tusa." May 28, 2011. lhanney.blogspot.com/2011/05/wasa-tusa.html.

Old Cowtown Museum Drug Store.

Salina Journal. "Seelye Mansion Gardens and Museum." March 31, 2005, 40.

Seeley Genealogical Society. "Alfred Barns Seelye." www.seeley-society.org/genealogy/biographies/alfred-barns-seelye/.

Seelye Mansion & Patent Medicine Museum. www.travelks.com/listing/seelye-mansion-%26-patent-medicine-museum/201/.

www.newspapers.com.

Tom Feist—Feist Publications

AP. "Feist Is Leaving Spearville." www.dodgeboard.com/forums/index.php?threads/feist-is-leaving-spearville.3182/.

Manhattan Mercury. "Small Town Readies for Loss of Phonebook Plant." March 12, 2007, 3.

Pemberton, Tricia. "City Branch of the Feist Family Enjoys Directory Business Role." *The Oklahoman*, February 29, 2004.

Salina Journal. "Kansas Lawyer Argues in Supreme Court." January 11, 1991, 3.

Tom Feist, 1933–2011. Obituary. www.zieglerfuneralchapel.com/obituary/1044729.

Wilson, Bill. "Feist Publications Patriarch Dies at 77." *Wichita Eagle*, January 20, 2011.

www.newspapers.com.

Norton County Meteorite

Arizona State University Center for Meteorite Studies. "Norton County Meteorite." meteorites.asu.edu/meteorites/norton-county.

Foster, Chris. "What He Brought in to the Antiques Road Show Is Literally Out of This World!" Dusty Old Thing. dustyoldthing.com/norton-county-meteorite/.

Lincoln, La Paz, Mathematician, Meteorite Hunter, Astronomer. www.angelfire.com/indie/anna_jones1/lapaz.html.

Michael Farmer Meteorites. www.meteoriteguy.com/catalog/nortoncounty.htm.

UNM Newsroom. "UNM's Institute of Meteoritics to Celebrate 75th Anniversary." September 5, 2019. news.unm.edu/news/unms-institute-of-meteoritics-to-celebrate-75th-anniversary.

Lyman Frank Baum

Biography. "Lyman Frank Baum Biography." April 12, 2014. www.biography.com/writer/l-frank-baum.

Debenedette, Valerie. "15 Wonderful Things You Might Not Know about L. Frank Baum." *Mental Floss*, May 15, 2018.

Encyclopaedia Britannica. "L. Frank Baum." www.britannica.com/biography/L-Frank-Baum.

Kansapedia. "Wizard of Oz." www.kshs.org/kansapedia/wizard-of-oz/12240.

Map of Kansas Literature. "L. Frank Baum." washburn.edu/reference/cks/mapping/baum/index.html.

McGovern, Linda. "L. Frank Baum—The Man Behind the Curtain." Literary Traveler, March 1, 1999. www.literarytraveler.com/articles/l-frank-baum-the-man-behind-the-curtain/.

Schama, Chloe. "Frank Baum, the Man behind the Curtain." *Smithsonian Magazine*, June 15, 2009.

Tanner, Beccy. "Wizard of Oz Linked Forever to Kansas." www.kansas.com/news/local/article1286945.html.

Taylor, Quentin P. "Money and Politics in the Land of Oz." *The Independent Review* 9, no. 3 (Winter 2004–05): 413–26.

Tallest Man in Congress

Burlingame Enterprise. "A Double Header." February 11, 1904, 3.

Find a Grave. "Daniel Reed Anthony, Jr." www.findagrave.com/.

Kansapedia. "Daniel R. Anthony, Jr." www.kshs.org/kansapedia/daniel-r-anthony-jr/16963.

Kansas Historical Society. Daniel Reed Anthony Jr. Papers. www.kshs.org/p/daniel-read-anthony-jr-papers/13974.

Morgan, P.W. "Daniel Reed Anthony." *The Kansas Chief,* April 6, 1916, 371.

Cordell, Kansas—Tornados Hit Three Years in a Row

Concordia Daily Kansan. "Cyclone Lays Town of Cordell Flat." May 22, 1918, 1.

Islandnet.com. "Three Strikes on Cordell." May 6, 2006. www.islandnet.com/~see/weather/almanac/arc2006/alm06may.htm.

Ottawa World. "An Old-Fashioned Kansas Twister." May 23, 1918, 6.

Quad-City Times (Davenport, IA). "Random Kinds of Factness." May 20, 2005, 23.

Soldier Clipper (Soldier, KS). "Kansas Tornado Kills Ten." May 29, 1918, 6.

Wilson, Ron. "Kansas Profile—Now That's Rural: Cordell—Cyclone Day, Part 2." www.ksre.k-state.edu/news/stories/2018/05/Kansas-Profile-Cordell-Tornados2.html.

———. "Tornado Strikes Town on Same Day Three Years in a Row." *Manhattan Mercury,* May 6, 2018.

www.newspapers.com.

www.rookscounty.net/images/1916-cordell-tornado-l.pdf.

INDEX

ABOUT THE AUTHOR

*I*t would be a long process to figure out how many generations of Roger Ringer's family have preceded him in Kansas and the United States. On the paternal side, it would be about seven generations in the United States and four in Kansas. On the other side, it would be around eight in the United States and five in Kansas, with a German/Scot heritage. The Elliott side of the family goes all the way back to Scotland (Clan Elliott), with a colorful heritage and an interesting connection to Mary Queen of Scotts. The clan has a history of intrigue and warfare in the old country, and somewhere along the line in the United States they became Quakers.

On the maternal side, there have been six generations in the United States and four in Kansas. This side was mostly German and from nearby lands that were all a part of the Prussian Empire at one time. On the other side is a German heritage with a touch of English, with five generations in Kansas.

From an uncle known as John the Prophet Elliott, who translated the first Bible into Algonquian Indian in the early Northeast states in the 1600s (the Bible is in a museum in the Northeast and was a *Jeopardy!* question), to an uncle Major Joel Elliott who died when Custer abandoned him and seventeen troopers at the Battle of the Washita during the attack on Black Kettle's camp, you might say that Roger is steeped in history.

Although he originally only wanted to be a farmer/rancher, life took twists and turns, with Roger becoming a firefighter/EMT with the Sedgwick County Fire District Number One. Retiring with a disability, he went on to become a private detective, auctioneer, realtor, welder, carpenter, cowboy, poet, township road boss, township trustee, writer and historian.

Roger has always had a wide range of interests and held many jobs, always meeting new people. And along the way, with an interest in rural issues, he started to get stories told to him everywhere he went.

With a downturn of health, most of the things that he loved he could no longer do. Rather than sit around and feel sorry for himself, he started to recall all the stories told to him over the years about Kansas. Since he had done some freelance writing and had a couple of manuscripts on the shelf, he turned to researching the stories. Roger found what he already knew—that Kansans are an industrious, ingenious and ornery people. Before he knew it, he had a manuscript he pitched to The History Press. They loved it, but it was way too long. This is now book three from that original work.

Be assured, this is not the last book. There are files upon files and topics listed on several pages of a notebook—and the list is added to every day.

Roger has also written an opinion column/blog since 2012 that is published in numerous newspapers, the most loyal being the *Rural Messenger*, a regional paper that covers the central section of Kansas.

There is work on other projects planned.